D1179198

SAMPLERS

HOW TO CREATE YOUR OWN DESIGNS

SAMPLERS

HOW TO CREATE YOUR OWN DESIGNS

JULIA MILNE

THE APPLE PRESS

A QUINTET BOOK

Published by The Apple Press
6 Blundell Street
London, N7 9BH

Copyright © 1989 Quintet Publishing Limited.
All rights reserved. No part of this publication
may be reproduced, stored in a retrieval system
or transmitted in any form or by any means,
electronic, mechanical, photocopying,
recording or otherwise, without the permission
of the copyright holder.

ISBN 1-85076-166-3

Reprinted 1991

This book was designed and produced by
Quintet Publishing Limited
6 Blundell Street
London N7 9BH

Creative Director: Peter Bridgewater
Art Director: Ian Hunt
Designer: James Lawrence
Editor: Caroline Beattie
Photographer: Andrew Sydenham
Illustrations: Julia Milne, Nicki Simmonds

Typeset in Great Britain by
Central Southern Typesetters, Eastbourne
Manufactured in Hong Kong by
Regent Publishing Services Limited
Printed in Hong Kong by
Leefung-Asco Printers Limited

CREDITS

Designs by Brenda Keyes for Country Yarns (available as kits from 13 Litchfield Drive, Prestwich, Manchester, England) appear on pages *36, 53, 54 (middle), 64, 66, 70, 74, 79*. Designs by Jane Greenoff for the Inglestone Collection (available as kits from Milton Place, Fairford, Gloucestershire, England) appear on pages *11, 14, 15, 48 (top), 63, 76, 77, 90, 91, 69 (bottom left)*. American Museum, Bath *8*. Fitzwilliam Museum, Cambridge *71 (left)*. Angelo Hornak Picture Library *12, 13*. The Danish House *48 (bottom)*. Victoria & Albert Museum *9, 10 (top), 49*.

CONTENTS

SAMPLERS IN
HISTORY

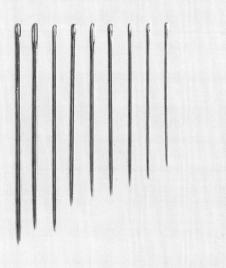

T HE HISTORY of European embroidery is a long and illustrious one with every conceivable surface having been embellished with the art of needlework. Garments and items of all kinds for both religious and domestic use were richly embroidered. During the Reformation in the 16th century, which involved the dissolution of English monasteries, many of the church vestments were burnt. That, coupled with the general wear and tear on domestic items, resulted in few early examples of European embroidery surviving. Those examples that do survive show us what a highly developed art embroidery was. These European traditions in needlework were taken to America during the 17th century by the early settlers and there is a great similarity in both the style and motifs used between early American embroidery and its European counterpart.

In the medieval period up to the end of the 14th century, English embroidery was considered to be the best in Europe and was known as *opus anglicanum* (English work). It was carried out by guilds of craftsmen and women who were mostly centred on monastic houses and medieval convents. Made solely for the Church and exported throughout Europe, its importance is shown by the fact that many of the best artists, who worked on the books and illuminated manuscripts, were also employed to design these great works of embroidered art.

On the domestic front it was mainly the women of noble houses and their servants who stitched the garments and items used in daily life. No well-born girl would have been considered a lady without being able to sew; all the Queens of Europe were well skilled with their needle. The Spanish Catherine of Aragon, Mary Queen of Scots educated in France and Elizabeth I of England were all noted for their skill at embroidery.

Although embroidery is considered to be a woman's art there were men who were employed as embroiderers in Royal households.

Queen Elizabeth of York, wife to Henry VII, employed one Robynet, who was paid £2 a year by the Privy Purse. Mary Queen of Scots, who embroidered away the hours of her long imprisonment, employed Pierre Oudry between 1560–67 and later Charles Plouvart as her embroiderers. The popularity of embroidery and the demand for rich and sumptious garments became so great in medieval Europe that there were various attempts to control what was seen as an excessive desire for finery. Edward III in 1363 decreed that:

"no one whose income was below four hundred marks per annum should wear cloth of gold or embroidery." ENGLISH SECULAR EMBROIDERY, M JOURDAIN PAGE 14

Later in 1586 a petition was presented to Catherine de Medici of France on *The Extreem Dearness of Living,* which declaimed that:

"mills, lands, pastures, woods, and all the revenues are wasted on embroideries, insertions, trimmings, tassels, fringes, hangings, gimps, needleworks, small chain stitchings, quiltings, back stitchings, etc: new diversities of which are invented daily". SAMPLERS AND TAPESTRY EMBROIDERIES. M B HUISH PAGE 12.

Below: *Spot sampler thought to be 19th century from Pennsylvania but showing the influence of the more subdued German samplers. The piece is worked entirely in cross stitch with a limited colour range.*

Right: *English sampler worked in 1656. This section shows traditional rose and carnation motifs and is worked in Montenegrin stitch, a version of long-armed cross stitch.*

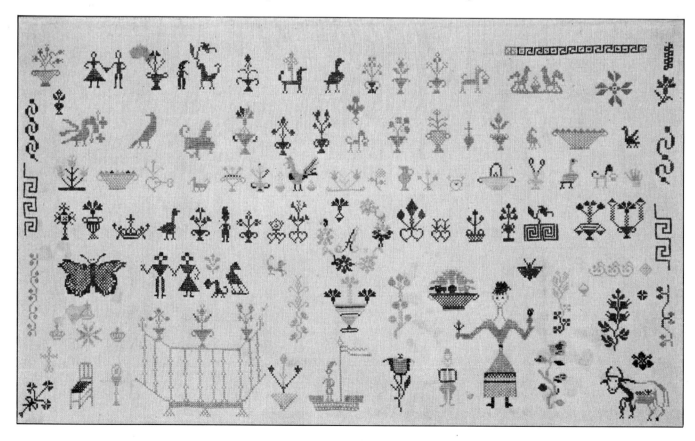

Samplers begin to make an appearance in the history of European embroidery from about the beginning of the 16th century although as long as people have embellished and embroidered cloth it is reasonable to suppose that they have made use of a sampler. In essence a sampler is a piece of cloth with diverse patterns and stitches used as a personal reference source. It is also an easy way to experiment with embroidery before starting a major project. Samplers appear in various European countries all at the same time with a great similarity in style and motifs used but there are some notable national differences. Italian samplers show a preference for cut and drawn thread work which seems to be influenced by the lace pattern books that were printed in Venice. Spanish samplers have bright colours and geometric designs perhaps related to the Moorish influence on Spanish decorative arts. German samplers are more restrained in colour and patterns whilst Delft vases can be found in Dutch examples. However, cross stitch is always the main embroidery technique used.

The earliest surviving sampler in England is one from the late 16th century worked by Jane Bostocke in 1598 to commemorate the birth of one Alice Lee but there is sufficient evidence to show that they were a common and useful tool before this date. The earliest mention of a sampler in England is in 1502 as an item in the Privy Purse expenses for that year which refers to a piece of linen cloth bought for Elizabeth of York as '. . . a sampler for the Queen.' Later in 1546 Margaret Thomson of Freestone in Lincolnshire bequeathed in her will, '. . . to Alys Pynchebeck my systers daughter my sampler with seams.' In 1552 in a household inventory of Edward VI there are two entries relating to samplers: one being a '. . . sampler of Normandie canvas wroughte with green and black silk . . . and a sampler and book of parchment containing diverse patternes.' These written records show that sampler making was carried out by the Queen and her ladies of the court and that samplers were imported from continental Europe. These were also important enough in themselves to be recorded. In an age when books were costly and rare the sampler, which was a personal book of patterns and stitches, would have been a valuable item worth passing on to the next generation.

Samplers were also mentioned in literature, an interesting example being in Shakespeare's *A Midsummers Night's Dream*, where reference is made to a sampler being stitched by two people. These are Helena's words to Hermia:

> *. . . O! Is all forgot?*
> *All school-days' friendship, childhood innocence?*
> *We, Hermia, like two artificial gods,*
> *Have with our needles created both one flower,*
> *Both on one sampler, sitting on one cushion,*
> *Both warbling of one song, both in one key,*
> *As if our hands, our sides, voices and minds,*
> *Had been incorporate.'* ACT 3 SCENE II

The above quote also seems to imply that samplers were made in childhood. Girls were taught to sew very early on in life and probably

Opposite, above: *English sampler worked by Elizabeth Macket in 1696 which is an example of a band sampler. It is worked in silk and linen thread on a linen ground and features rose, carnation, grape and vine leaf motifs. The stitches used include cross, Italian cross, double running, satin and rococo stitch.*

Opposite, below: *Section of an American alphabet sampler made by Nabby Ford in 1799 showing the freer floral border worked in crewel wools that is typical of the American style. The borders became increasingly more elaborate until the central panels became dwarfed by the foliage.*

Left: *Birth Sampler (32cm × 26cm/13in × 10¼in). The oldest dated sampler in England was worked by Jane Bostocke in 1598 to commemorate the birth of a girl and this is a contemporary version of a traditional gift. In the 16th century a sampler was a valuable item to give to a child and although today girls no longer need to know how to sew, you could still pass on your favourite motifs and patterns to the next generation.*

did make samplers; however, due to the high standard of workmanship it is generally considered that the surviving examples of early samplers were made by adult needlewomen. It is unlikely, prior to the 16th century, that samplers would have been worked by women of all classes: the cost of materials was high (linen cloth and silk thread have always been expensive) and this type of decorative embroidery was probably only worked by wealthy ladies with time on their hands.

In Europe and America the early samplers are known as 'band samplers', which are long thin strips of linen generally three times longer than the width. They appear to have been made from the end of a length of cloth as they mostly have selvedges at the top and bottom with the long sides being hemmed. The patterns on them are worked in bands long enough to show the repeat plus 'spot' motifs such as birds, flowers and animals. These band samplers were also a convenient size and shape to use as a reference source as they could be rolled up and stored easily in a work box.

The shape and content of samplers changed gradually during the 17th century until in the 18th century they take on the more familiar square shape with spot motifs and inscriptions. These are generally referred to a spot samplers. By this time the sampler had ceased to be a personal book of stitches and become either an exercise in sewing competence produced by young girls or simply an embroidered picture made to be displayed in a frame. There has never been a standard shape or size for a sampler and over the centuries any piece of left over cloth has been used. It was not until 1882 when sampler making had virtually ceased to exist that Canlfield and Sawards' *Dictionary of Needlework* gave written instructions as to what a sampler should be both in terms of its size and design content.

The patterns and motifs found in early samplers tend to be fairly similar from one to another which suggests that they were traditional designs passed on from one generation to the next. From the first half of the 16th century printed pattern books, as design sources for embroiderers, begin to appear in Europe. They were from presses either in Germany, Italy or France and proved so popular that many were reprinted in several editions. One of the most influential of these books was *Schön Neues Modelbuch* published by Johann Sibmacher in Nurnberg in 1597, which was later reproduced in England as *The Needles Excellency*. Richard Shorleykers' *A Scholehouse for the*

Right *A traditional 19th-century Greek band sampler. The left-hand sampler shows patterns worked in cross stitch which were probably used to embroider shirts and blouses; the right band includes cross, satin, running and Holbein stitch with some couching.*

Opposite *Verse sampler finished by Anne Brasher in the eleventh year of her life on March 3rd 1789. It is decorated with a wild strawberry border and flower and animal motifs. This sampler also includes an unusual boat motif which appears as a high-backed galleon typical of the 16th and 17th centuries. A man on deck seems to be flying a kite. Stitches used include cross, stem and satin stitch.*

Against Idleness

I

How doth the little busy Bee
Improve each shining Hour
And gather Honey all the Day
From every opening Flower

II

How skilfully she builds her cell
How neat she spreads the wax
And labours hard to store it well
With the sweet Food she makes

And Mischief

III

In Works of Labour or of Skill
I would be busy too   still
For Satan finds some Mischief
For idle Hands to do

IV

In Books Work or healthful play
Let my first Years be past
That I may give for every Day
Some good Account at last

Ann Brasher Finished this Sampler in the Eleventh year
of her Age March the third 1789

Above: *Map sampler (42cm ×
35cm/16½in × 13¾in). A modern
version of a map sampler. These map
samplers were popular in Europe
during the 18th century and served to
teach girls geography while learning
their embroidery. This example is
worked in cross stitch with the county
names in running stitch, each county
is outlined in a different colour to its
neighbour's following the practice on
printed maps.*

Needle, also published around this time, was full of fruit, flower and leaf spray motifs but more importantly it was the first book to give instructions for enlarging or reducing the size of a design by using a squared grid, a simple and efficient method still used today. The patterns in these books were not necessarily original as there was no copyright law to stop the practice of borrowing designs from all sorts of sources. Motifs used in American samplers prior to the 18th century can be traced back to these European pattern books. Many English ladies went to settle in the new colonies and took their pattern books with them. Often they would make their living by teaching needlework and advertised themselves as having the latest designs from England.

During the 18th century pattern books lost favour with embroiderers in Europe as they tended to use printed fabrics as design sources and increasingly alphabets and moral verses replaced the more decorative spot or band patterns. By the mid 18th century pattern books were being published in America and many of the needlework teachers drew their own patterns and motifs for embroidery. This, coupled with the increasing population of America and the associated need to develop a more refined culture, led to the distinctive American style in samplers. While European samplers were becoming more rigid in content and style, the American ones became freer and more pictorial. Houses and landscapes became the preferred subject for samplers and a variety of materials such as beads, hair, ribbons and even paper were added to the wool or linen background to increase the surface interest. From this point on these American samplers should really be considered as embroidered pictures.

Sewing was an important part of any girl's education: it was a necessary accomplishment for a young lady and for less fortunate girls good sewing skills would at least afford them reasonable employment. From the 17th century onwards the sampler became a means of not only teaching girls how to sew but also a certificate of their competence. Their importance was not lost on teachers and the inclusion of inscriptions and verses served to give the girls a moral education. Later on the craze for map samplers combined the teaching of geography with needlework. These schoolgirl samplers were produced in vast numbers and show the high level of skill achieved by even very young girls.

During the 19th century there was a steady decline in the practice of sampler making as other forms of needlework took over in popularity. Knitting, crochet and tatting were all favoured and popularized by the new magazines aimed at women. Books on needlework became cheap and plentiful and cloth printed with a design ready to stitch were also available. In the middle of the 19th century the sewing machine was invented and the need to teach girls how to sew by hand ceased to be important which led to a sharp decline in sampler making. Nowadays there is a renewed interest in the art of sampler making and many individuals and museums realize the importance of collecting these unique documents of social history.

Right: *The River Thames (76cm × 16cm/29¾in × 6¼in). An interesting contemporary working of a map sampler where all areas of interest along the river are marked with a relevant motif. Any river or road map sampler could be worked in this way and a local area or favourite walk might be added in to a sampler.*

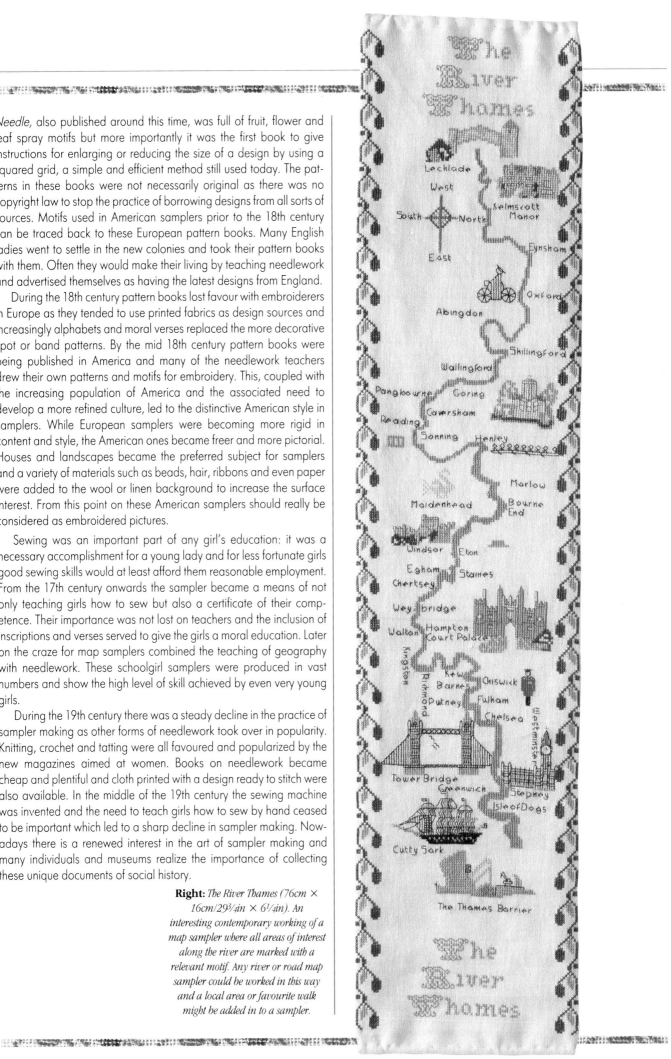

STITCHES, MATERIALS AND WORKING WITH
DESIGNS

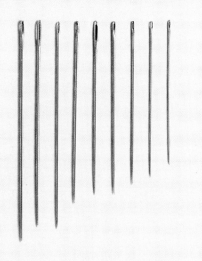

Above: *Alphabet and House sampler worked by Julia Sargeant aged 9 in 1829 and thought to be made in Vermont. The verse and alphabet are more in the European tradition while the landscape at the bottom shows the American fashion for pictorial scenes. Worked in silk on a linen ground using cross stitch and satin stitch.*

Above: *A rare American Indian sampler from the 18th century, possibly Chippewa, from the Great Lakes area. It is worked in chain on a linen ground. The heart motifs in the corners are European in origin but the animal designs are Indian. The central panel of four birds and a fish are surrounded by two larger birds, a moose and a long-tailed animal that may represent a panther or similar cat. It is a unique combination of design traditions from two cultures. Its use is unclear although it seems likely that it was made as a gift for a white person.*

STITCHES

THERE ARE many embroidery stitches that, over the centuries, have been used in sampler making and a good stitch encyclopedia will show all the different types of basic and decorative stitches. Included here are some of the more common stitches used in sampler making with a selection of interesting fancy stitches made up from the basic ones. There are a sufficient number of stitches illustrated here to help you design and create any kind of sampler.

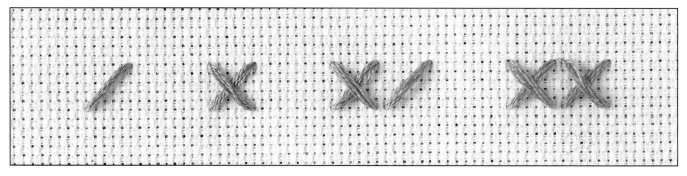

◆ Cross Stitch ◆

Also known as sampler stitch due to the vast number of samplers worked entirely in this stitch. It is probably the best known of all embroidery stitches and can be found in examples of embroidery all over the world. It is a quick and simple stitch to work, especially on even weave fabric or canvas where the number of threads can be counted to keep the size of the stitches even. There are two basic methods for working cross stitch but in both the direction of the top diagonal stitches should all fall the same way, unless the effect in light and shade is desired.

Individual cross stitch is worked as a complete cross before going onto the next stitch and is best suited to canvas work or for outlining shapes in embroidery. Cross stitch worked in rows is best suited to filling in large areas. Here one row of diagonals is worked in one direction followed by the second row of diagonals, to form the crosses, worked in the opposite direction.

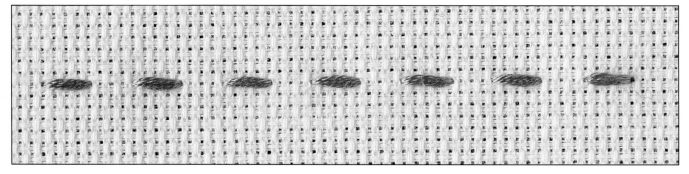

◆ Running Stitch ◆

The simplest and most basic of all embroidery stitches. It is made by passing the thread in and out of the fabric at regular intervals making sure that the stitches and spaces are the same length. Mostly used for fine linear detail.

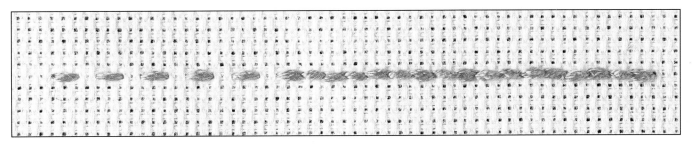

◆ Holbein Stitch ◆

Also known as double running stitch, this is a very old and simple line stitch used a lot in samplers to outline motifs. Its name derives from a particular use of the stitch on shirts, collars and cuffs in the 16th century recorded in portraits by the painter Hans Holbein (1497–1543). The stitch is formed by working a row of even spaced running stitches and the spaces in between are filled in with running stitch on the return journey. This makes an even, linear stitch that is the same on both sides. A variation is to step the stitches to give a zig-zag line.

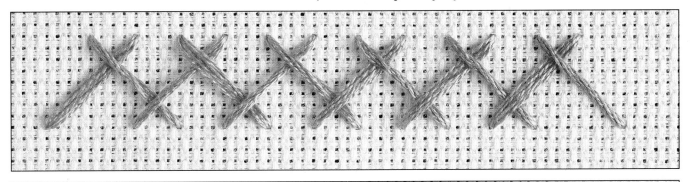

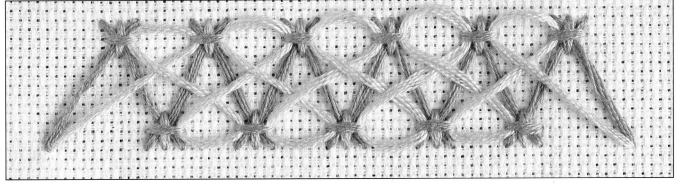

◆ Herringbone Stitch and Fancy Herringbone ◆

Herringbone stitch is a simple stitch formed much in the same way as individual cross stitch except that the width of the stitch is always less than the height to form an off-centre cross. Basic herringbone can be used as a foundation for more complex stitches such as fancy herringbone where, after a foundation row of herringbone is worked, small vertical and horizontal cross stitches are worked over the herringbone crosses, and these crosses are then interlaced with a third thread. In this simple manner a seemingly complex and interesting border can be worked.

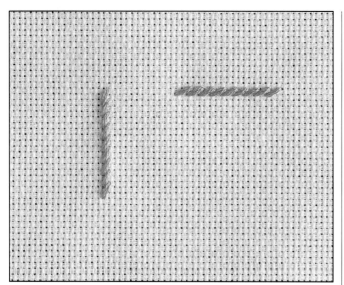

◆ Stem Stitch ◆

This is a simple line stitch used to outline shapes and details. The stitch is worked with a simple forwards and backwards motion along the line to be embroidered. The working thread should be kept to the right of the stitches.

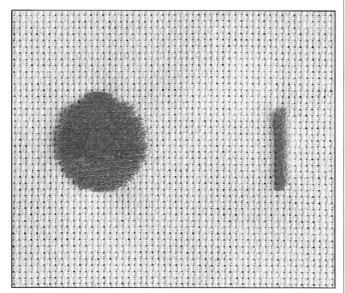

◆ Satin Stitch ◆

This is another very old stitch found in embroidery all around the world which can be used as a line stitch or filling stitch. It should always be worked on fabric stretched in an embroidery hoop. It is made up of straight stitches worked side by side and the stitches should always lie evenly and cover the fabric entirely. When it is used as a line stitch it is generally worked at a slight angle to the direction of the line, when used as a filling stitch the whole shape is covered with either vertical or horizontal lines to give an effect of light and shade. Long satin stitches can be difficult to keep even so it is best to use it on small shapes;

larger areas can be covered with LONG AND SHORT STITCH. This is a variation of satin stitch where the first row of stitches are worked alternately in long and short stitches that follow the outline of the shape to be covered. The rest of the area is covered in satin stitches equal in length to the long stitches.

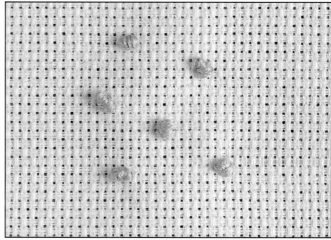

◆ French Knots ◆

These are small individual stitches mostly used to create texture. Any weight of yarn can be used to give different-sized stitches and the number of twists round the needle can be altered to give a large or small knot. The stitch is worked by bringing the thread through to the right side, inserting just the *point* of the needle in and out of the fabric where the thread emerges, twisting the yard round the needle two or three times, then inserting the needle back through the same hole. The yard is pulled through the twists to form the knot. It is always easier to work this stitch with the fabric held in a frame and with a little practice even-sized knots can be achieved.

◆ Algerian Eye Stitch ◆

This is made by working eight stitches all into a central point as though following the outline of a square. It forms a star-shaped stitch and if the threads are pulled a little more tightly than usual a small hole forms at the centre of each star.

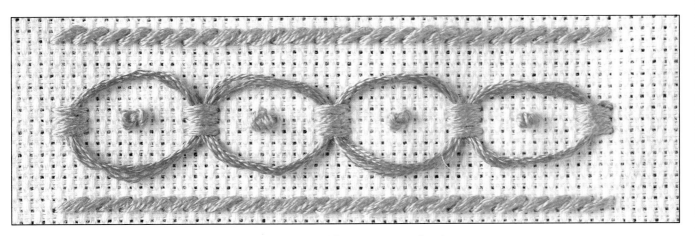

◆ Guilloche Stitch ◆

This is a composite stitch made up from three basic stitches to form an interesting border. First two parallel rows of stem stitch are worked, then three short satin stitches are formed at regular intervals between the rows of stem stitch. These are then interlaced together with a third thread worked in two journeys of alternate semi-circles to form circles in between the satin stitches. A French knot is worked in the centre of each circle.

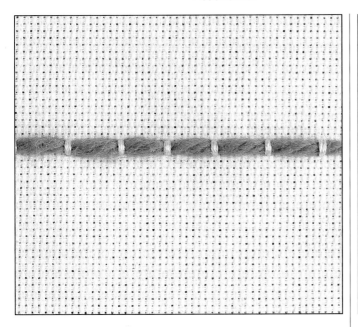

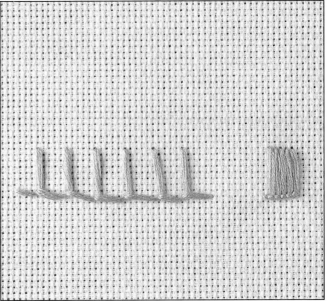

◆ Couching ◆

This is found mainly on early samplers as couching was used extensively in medieval embroidery to make the best use of precious gold and silver thread. It is a simple method of catching down a metal thread or a much thicker yarn without having to take it through the fabric. The fabric must be held in an embroidery frame. Bring the yarn to be laid down through to the front, then using a much finer matching yarn, catch down the laid thread by using small straight stitches at intervals over the laid thread. When the line or shape that is to be couched is finished the thread is taken back to the wrong side.

◆ Buttonhole Stitch and Blanket Stitch ◆

These two stitches are worked in exactly the same way: it is the variation in the closeness of the stitches that gives rise to the different names. In blanket stitch a space is left between each upright and in buttonhole stitch they lie next to each other. Both stitches are worked from left to right by working a straight stitch down the fabric and over the working thread, so that a row of vertical stitches are joined together by a looped stitch at the bottom. As their names suggest, both these stitches are often used to finish off raw edges.

◆ Torocko Stitch ◆

A simple but effective stitch built up in three stages and best worked in three colours with the fabric stretched on a frame. First work a grid of long stitches, then into each alternate square work an upright cross stitch, to finish work short diagonal stitches over the centre of the upright crosses so as to couch them down.

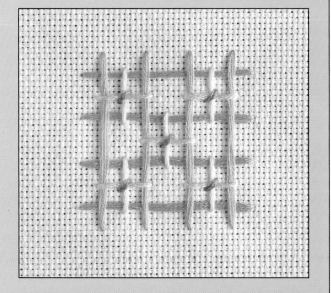

◆ Squared Filling Stitch ◆

Another composite stitch made up of three simple ones and similar to work as torocko stitch. This time work a double grid of long stitches on the diagonal, couch down the intersections with a small upright cross stitch and finish with a French knot worked in the centre of each diamond.

◆ Trellis Couching ◆

This is a decorative stitch that makes a solid covered area. It is best worked in two or three colours and must be worked with the help of an embroidery frame for a successful result. The area to be filled is covered with straight stitches like satin stitches but worked alternately in one direction with the spaces filled in on the return. Over this a trellis is laid and couched down at the intersection of the trellis with a small straight stitch. This is a stitch for experienced embroiderers.

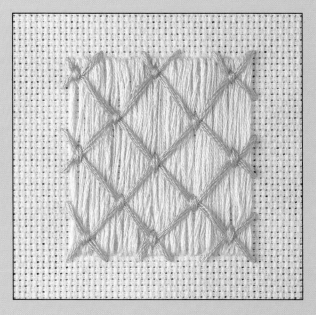

MATERIALS

◆ Fabrics ◆

The traditional fabric for samplers was linen, generally a piece cut off a length of fabric which could vary from coarse unbleached to fine pillowcase linen. The threads used were either linen or twisted silk although some of the earliest surviving examples have gold and silver

Below: *A selection of general embroidery equipment and materials. Plain weave fabric, white and cream even-weave fabric, embroidery frame, needles, scissors, marking pencils, wool and cotton threads.*

thread as well. The early samplers were used as pattern books rather than merely decorative pieces so the threads used were probably those left over from some larger piece of work.

When samplers became more popular as a teaching method, the linen, which was expensive, was substituted with a woollen 'tammy cloth' made especially for sampler making. The thread used was usually silk although crewel wool is also found on coarser examples. The woollen cloth has not lasted as well as the more expensive linen as it tends to attract moths and generally disintegrates more quickly. At the beginning of the 19th century linen and linen canvas were used once more but once the craze for Berlin woolwork started on cotton canvas, sampler making very quickly lost its former popularity.

Today there are other alternative fabrics for sampler making. Linen is still available and is always the best choice for an experienced stitcher, but cotton Aida cloth, particularly the finer gauges such as 18 holes to the inch, is a better choice for beginners, and the less experienced. On Aida cloth the threads can be counted and the stitches kept to a regular size, particularly cross stitch, which is the basic stitch for most samplers. Fine quality silk or cotton threads are most suitable and readily available in large shade ranges; linen threads and metallic threads are also available from most good embroidery shops. As with all handmade items, the better the quality of materials the better the finished result.

Fabrics fall into three main groups: plain weave, even weave and canvas, all of which are suitable for sampler making.

PLAIN WEAVE fabrics are those such as cotton, linen and wool with a regular tightly-woven stucture used for fine embroidery. Used in conjunction with an embroidery frame all types of stitches can be worked on plain weave fabrics.

EVEN WEAVE fabrics are similar to plain weave except that the warp and weft threads are of exactly the same thickness which gives a regular number of threads within a given area. This enables you to count the threads and work regular-sized stitches. The most useful fabrics are Hardanger, Binca and Aida cloth, all of which come in a variety of counts or threads to the inch and are made from cotton or cotton/synthetic blends. Pure cotton is always the preferred choice.

CANVAS is woven in different gauges to produce a fabric with precisely spaced holes. There is single or double thread canvas and as their name suggests there are either one or two threads between each hole. The stitches are formed between each hole and so generally only the finer gauges of canvas are suitable for sampler making in the traditional way, however a canvas work sampler can be worked showing different patterns and stitches without filling in the background. Canvas is commonly available in cotton or linen and in silk as a very fine gauze.

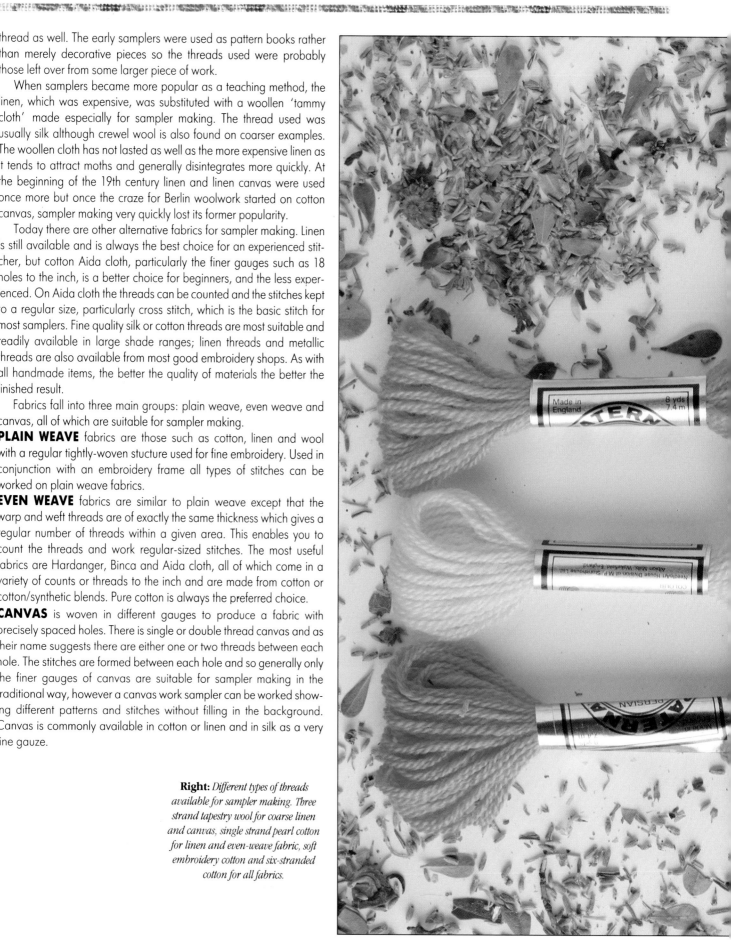

Right: *Different types of threads available for sampler making. Three strand tapestry wool for coarse linen and canvas, single strand pearl cotton for linen and even-weave fabric, soft embroidery cotton and six-stranded cotton for all fabrics.*

Above: *An enormous and exciting array of colours and yarns is available for embroidery. You will quickly find out which materials you prefer to work with.*

◆ Threads ◆

Threads for embroidery are available in a large range of weights and colours. There are basically two types, single twisted or stranded yarn. Single threads include *pearl cotton,* a twisted two-ply thread in a number of weights with a sheen finish, *coton à broder,* a high twist cotton which is softer and less shiny than pearl cotton and *soft embroidery cotton* which is a five-ply yarn with a matt finish. Stranded threads are either in cotton or silk. Cotton thread is a six-strand thread that can be divided to create different thicknesses of yarn for different weights of fabric. It has a high sheen finish and is the most versatile of all embroidery threads. Pure silk comes as a seven-strand thread which again can be sub-divided. It also has a high sheen and comes in a shade range that includes colours of a more brilliant hue.

◆ Needles and Frames ◆

Embroidery needles are readily available and have larger eyes than normal sewing needles to allow for the thicker threads. They come in many different sizes numbered from coarse (the low numbers) to fine (the high numbers). The exact number of a needle does not matter as long as the eye of the needle passes through the fabric with ease and does not distort or pucker the surface. Remember to use a sharp long-eyed needle for plain weave fabrics and a tapestry (blunt-ended) needle for even weave fabrics and canvas.

Embroidery frames come in a large selection of sizes and types and it is very much up to personal preference in the way that you work that will determine the size and style of frame to choose. There are two main types, hand held and freestanding. The easiest and most versatile of the hand held frames is the two-ring embroidery hoop, where the fabric is stretched and held taught between the two rings which are placed one on top of the other, the top one of which can be adjusted with a tension screw. The freestanding frames are more commonly used for canvas work, and here the canvas or fabric is stitched and laced onto a frame and held taught. The two-ring hoop is most often used for finer materials. One of each of these two types of frames will be sufficient for nearly all your embroidery projects.

WORKING WITH DESIGNS

The traditional method of transferring designs onto cloth for embroidery, before the advent of ready made transfers, was to outline the design with pinholes and then shake charcoal dust through the holes on to the fabric below. This is a method that you could use today by substituting tailor's chalk for the charcoal but it is rather a messy process and does result in pinholes through your favourite design. There are suitable alternatives.

◆ Dressmaker's Carbon Paper ◆

This is a quick and simple method of transferring a design onto a smooth plain or even weave fabric. First, using ordinary tracing paper, draw round the design to be transferred, then place this drawing over the right side of the fabric with a sheet of dressmaker's tracing paper, coloured side down, in between. Using a sharp pencil re-draw over the traced design making sure that the design registers on the fabric underneath. On light coloured fabrics use blue or red tracing paper; on darker fabrics white or yellow tracing paper is best.

Below: *Lily motif taken from an early 17th-century European pattern book. These motifs would have been transferred by outlining the design with pin holes and using charcoal dust to mark the design through the holes onto the fabric below.*

◆ Using a Light Box ◆

For fine fabrics or canvas the use of a light box is another easy way of transferring your designs. First trace round the design and then place it on a sheet of clear perspex or glass supported by two chairs. Place a strong light underneath the glass and position the fabric over the tracing. Secure the fabric and tracing to the glass with masking tape and using a sharp soft pencil draw the design as seen through the fabric. This method can also be used for transferring a line drawing onto graph paper which is particularly useful when you want to work a design in cross stitch. Simply place the graph paper over the traced design and following the lines of the design mark the corresponding squares on the graph paper.

◆ Enlarging a Design ◆

When working from a charted design, where one square represents one stitch, to enlarge or reduce the scale of the design you simply change the size of the stitches. This automatically changes the scale of the design but keeps it in the same proportions.

If the design you wish to use is not on a chart and you want to change the scale of the design the easiest way is to enlarge or reduce it by using a squared grid. First draw a grid over the design using lines 1 inch apart, then make an edge to the grid so that it is either square or rectangular. Place tracing paper over this grid and mark the bottom horizontal and left hand vertical lines to correspond with the grid below. Draw a diagonal line from the bottom left hand corner through the top right hand corner and extended as far as you want to enlarge the design to. Complete the square or rectangle by filling in the top horizontal and right hand vertical lines. Measure the width and height of the new square or rectangle and divide it by the same number of squares as the grid below. Reproduce the design by copying the lines within each square of the first grid into the larger squares of the second grid. The design will be enlarged but stay in the same proportions as before. To reduce a design work the same way but make the second grid smaller than the original.

Changing design size

1 *Enclose the design within a rectangle. Using letters and numbers to identify the lines, divide design into squares. Draw a diagonal line through design.*

2 *Place design on a large piece of paper in the bottom left corner and extend the diagonal line to height needed. Complete the rectangle and divide into same number of squares as original. Add letters and numbers.*

Above: *Illustrated here is a method of transferring a design by using dressmaker's carbon paper. A tracing is made from the original design; this tracing is then placed over dressmaker's carbon paper which is placed coloured side down onto the ground fabric. The design is then re-traced using a sharp pencil so that the motif registers on the fabric below. The design can now be embroidered. The lines are usually fine enough to be covered by the embroidery.*

Right: *Hand held embroidery frame or hoop set up with a traced design ready to work.*

DESIGNING YOUR OWN SAMPLER

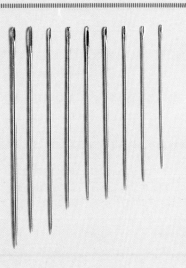

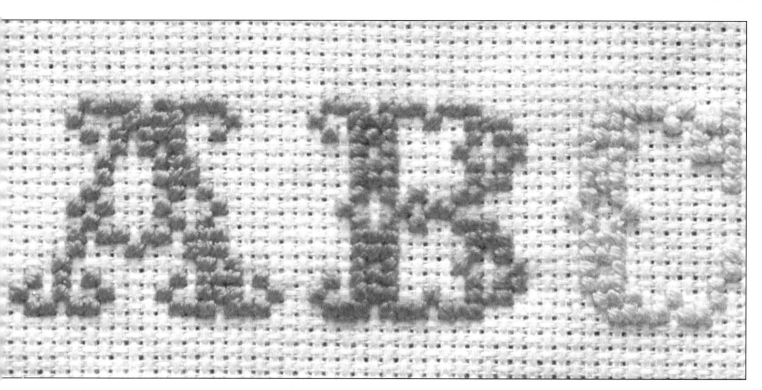

WHEN DESIGNING your own sampler, the first step is to decide what type of sampler it is going to be. A house, alphabet, spot or commemorative sampler could be worked along traditional lines or any combination of these ideas could be put into a contemporary sampler. Included in this book are many motifs and designs from samplers worked over the past few hundred years which you can use as a design source. However you could also build up your own library of patterns culled from other sources.

Having decided on the motifs and style of the sampler, the next stage is to choose the ground fabric and threads that you are going to use. An experienced embroiderer can choose from a wide range of materials but for a beginner an even-weave fabric with no more than 18 holes to an inch and a single thread yarn would be the best choice. Even-weave fabric helps to keep the stitches regular and if the gauge is not too fine a reasonable result can be achieved quite quickly. A single thread yarn is easier to handle than a six strand thread and again helps to keep the stitches regular. A sampler can be any size or shape but for a first attempt a piece of fabric around 12 x 13 in/30 x 35 cms would be a good size to fit most patterns and motifs.

Before starting the embroidery the design could be planned out on a piece of graph paper. Using one square on the graph to represent one stitch the whole design can be charted before starting and the motifs and verses places as desired. This will give you a more considered design, but as most samplers were made by very young girls without planning the design out in this way, this approach can lead to a loss of vitality in the finished piece of work. Much of the charm of samplers lies in the unexpected positioning of words and motifs and this is something that is difficult to plan.

One of the best ways to work a sampler, having sorted out the ground fabric, yarns and some favourite motifs, is to just start. A border could be a starting place or even a large central motif around which other patterns and ideas could be worked. In this fashion a naïve quality is kept in the work and the spacing can be unpredictable.

There is, after all, little that can go wrong with a sampler, as mistakes and imperfections will only add to the charm of the picture. Any haphazard placing of motifs and designs can be unified and turned into a complete piece of work by the addition of a simple border. Work the border in colours that have already been used in the sampler to give the piece of work a considered and finished look. Last but not least sign and date your work for the social historians of the future.

These pages: *Contemporary sampler (with details) made by the author using motifs and stitches shown in this book.*

Birth Samplers

Above *A modern birth sampler worked in cross stitch to commemorate the birth of a girl.*

Right *A contemporary birth sampler kit. It includes trains, buses, cars, and boat motifs and is worked in tent stitch using wool on a cotton canvas.*

Valentine Motifs

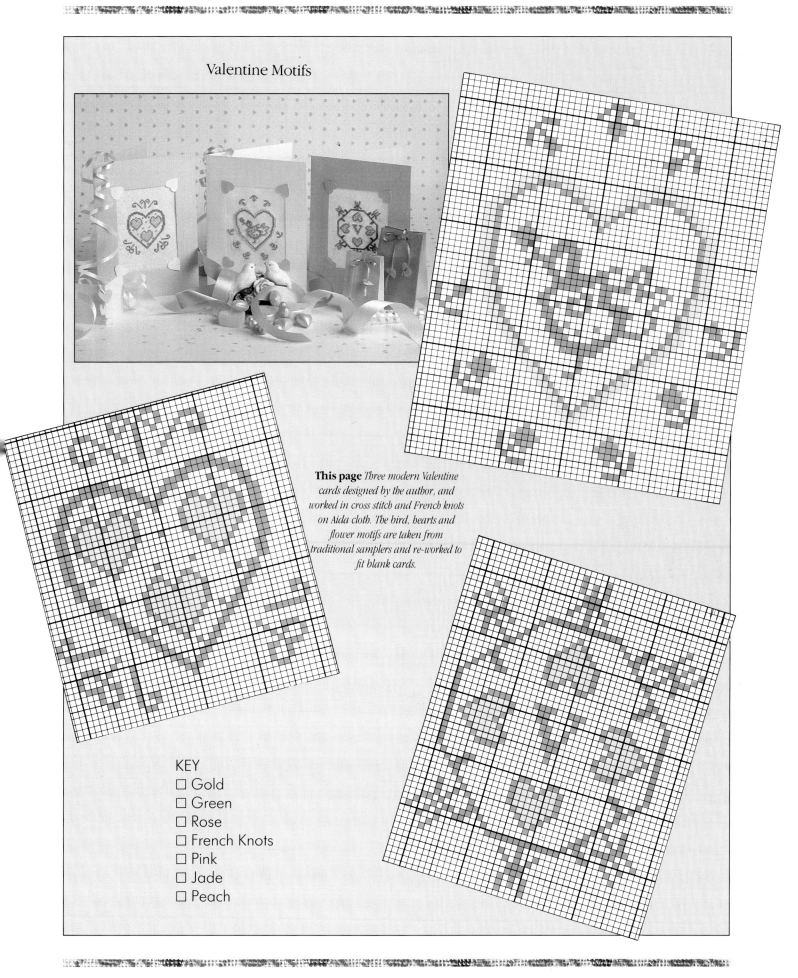

This page *Three modern Valentine cards designed by the author, and worked in cross stitch and French knots on Aida cloth. The bird, hearts and flower motifs are taken from traditional samplers and re-worked to fit blank cards.*

KEY
☐ Gold
☐ Green
☐ Rose
☐ French Knots
☐ Pink
☐ Jade
☐ Peach

FLOWERS, FRUITS AND TREES

Patterns of flowers, fruits and trees occur in all periods and types of embroidery and are found abundantly in virtually every sampler. Sometimes the flowers are depicted in a naturalistic way but mostly they are in a more abstract pattern form. In early samplers they were also used with specific reference to their symbolic meaning.

Various flowers have had symbolic meanings attached to them, most of which date from a pre-Christian era. These meanings were then adapted to fit in with Christian values and teachings. In a medieval world that was largely illiterate, the only means of education was through the Church. Wall paintings, stained glass windows and altar pieces would have given a visual education as the stories of the Bible were learnt through pictures. Fruits and flowers would have been used as part of this process of story telling and there would have been a general understanding of their symbolic meaning. The flowers most commonly used were the rose, carnation, lily, honeysuckle and strawberry, both fruit and flower.

The rose had an early pagan association with earthly love, but to the Christians it became the flower of heavenly or divine love and is often used in conjunction with the Virgin Mary. In samplers this association is also used with the notion that the rose is the flower of Tudor England. The carnation, which is very popular in samplers, has a simi-

lar meaning to the rose and the two are generally interchangeable. The lily, also known as the flower of heaven, was often used in pictures of the Annunciation and has come to symbolise purity or chastity.

The honeysuckle was a favourite flower of the Tudors and is much alluded to in Shakespeare as the eglantine or woodbine. At this time it grew freely in woodlands and its Christian symbolic meaning is of enduring faith. In country lore it has the reputation of warding off the evil eye and as such is a useful choice as a motif for any embroiderer.

The strawberry is a popular and enduring flower and fruit motif still much in evidence in contemporary samplers. It is now only generally shown in fruit form but in old samplers it is shown in both forms and has a special Christian relevance. 'Very perfect fruit with neither thorns nor stone but sweet, soft and delicious through and through. Its flowers are the whiteness of innocence and its leaves almost of the sacred trefoil form and since it grows along the ground, not on a tree, there is no possibility of it being the dread fruit of the tree of knowledge – its meaning is that of perfect righteousness.' Elizabeth Haig – Floral symbolism of the Great Masters.

Other popular flowers include the marigold, cowslip, violet, tulip and the pansy, which was reputed to be a favourite of Elizabeth I. In 17th century British samplers the thistle was often used to show the union of England and Scotland under James I & VI. Through the 18th and 19th centuries flowers and fruits tended to be used simply as decorative elements and are often shown in baskets and urns.

This page: *Drawings of flower motifs taken from an English sampler worked by Martha Wheeler in 1710. The flowers are all worked in satin stitch with some stem stitch and French knots. Once a drawing has been made from an original sampler the shape can then be traced round and transferred to the fabric for working. If you feel confident about drawing, motifs can be drawn straight onto the ground fabric with a soft pencil. Many designs were transferred by drawing freehand and it does give a lively and original quality to the motifs and subsequent embroidery.*

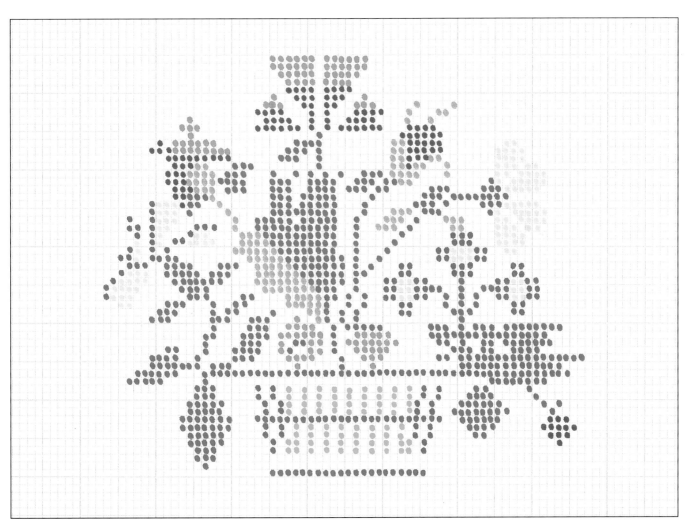

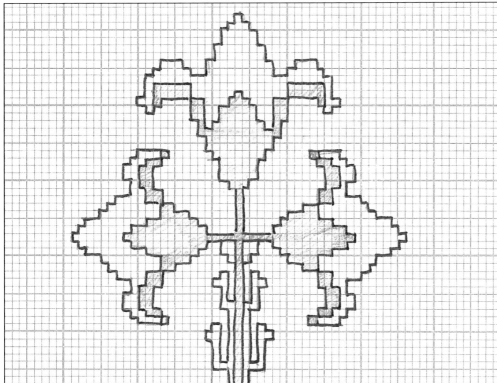

Above: *Baskets and urns full of flowers were popular in samplers and often figured larger than any other motif. This example is taken from a sampler dated 1840 and worked by Lucy Grant. She used silk thread on a wool ground and the colours shown here are the ones she chose to work the design in.*

Left: *A simple 18th-century lily motif which could be worked in cross stitch or more effectively embroidered in satin stitch using close tones of cream, yellow and light green.*

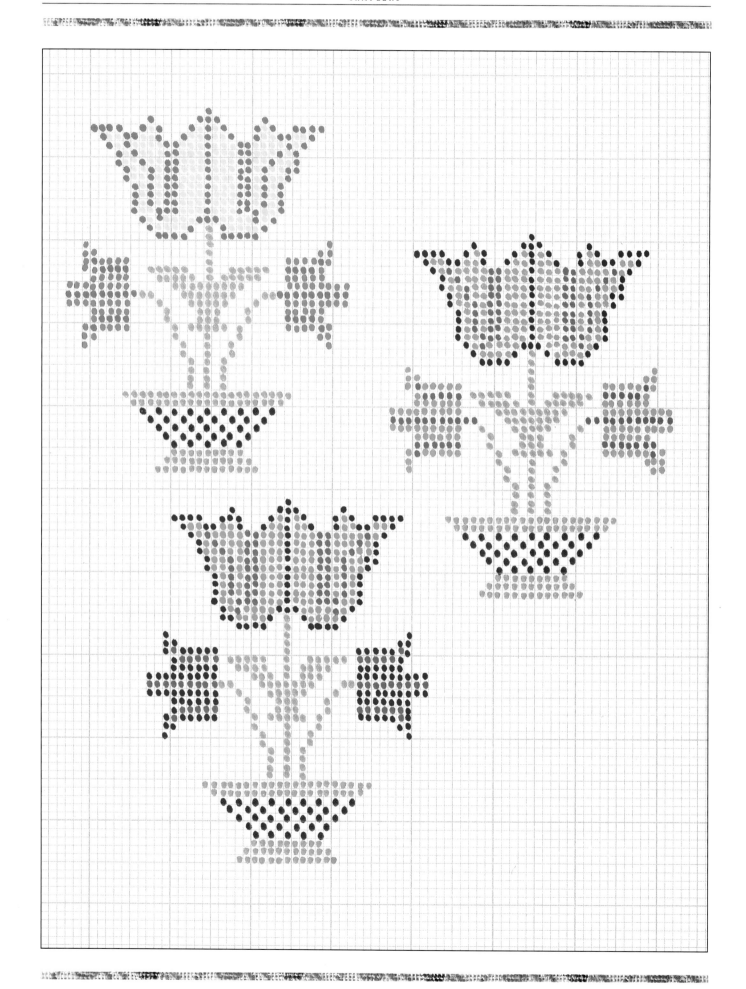

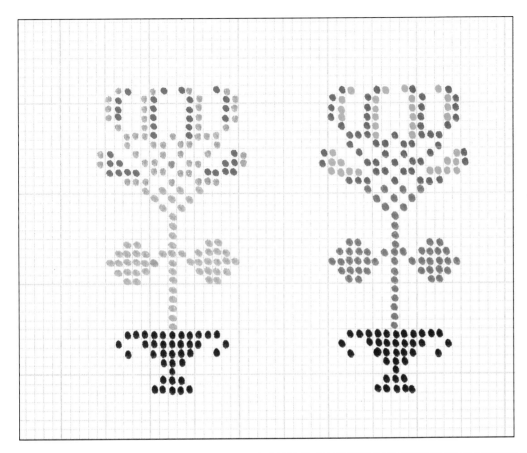

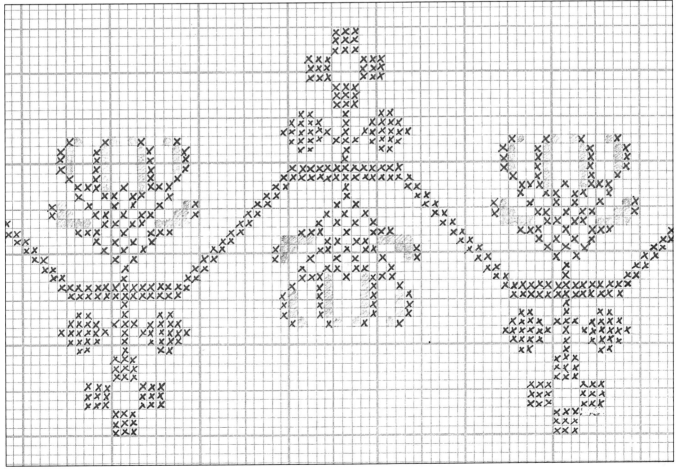

Opposite page: *A 19th-century tulip motif that has been taken from a black and white pattern book. Experiment with different colour combinations. The same motif has been worked out on a piece of graph paper using coloured crayons. If you are unsure of a colour for a design or wish to change it, the easiest way to decide on a new colour is to work the motif on paper with crayons; this way you can check the design before starting the embroidery.*

This page: *A honeysuckle and rose motif ready to work in cross stitch either as a border or individual motif placed in an urn. This example is from a 19th-century sampler but honeysuckle was popular as a motif through the preceding three centuries.*

These pages: *Flower motifs taken from the pattern book 'A Scholehouse for the needle', published in 1624 by Richard Shorleyker. This was the first embroidery book to explain how to enlarge or reduce a design by using the grid method.*

Right: *Rose and urn motif from an 18th-century sampler worked in cross stitch. The flowers in these motifs always seem to dwarf the pot or vase that they stand in. These motifs are found in samplers throughout America and Europe.*

Below: *This rose motif is taken from an 18th-century sampler where it was worked entirely in cross stitch. Here the design has been placed directly onto graph paper where one square represents one full cross stitch.*

Right: *An assortment of fruit and flower baskets and urns taken from 18th-century samplers. They could be used as individual motifs to fill a space on a large sampler or grouped all together to form a spot sampler.*

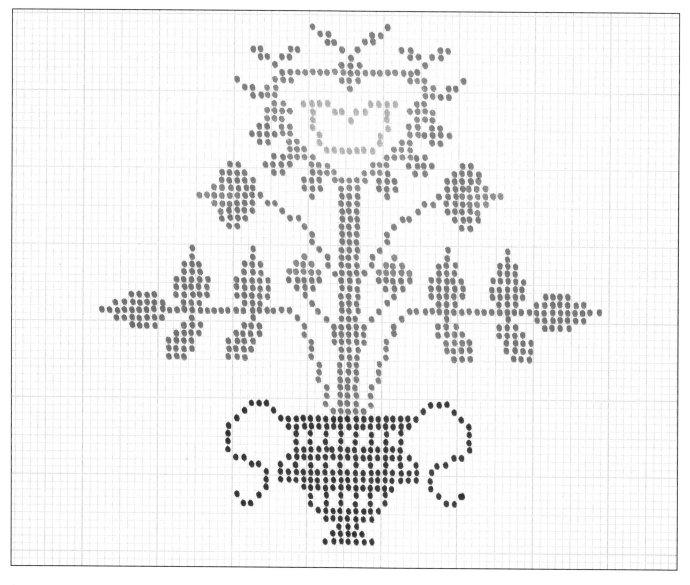

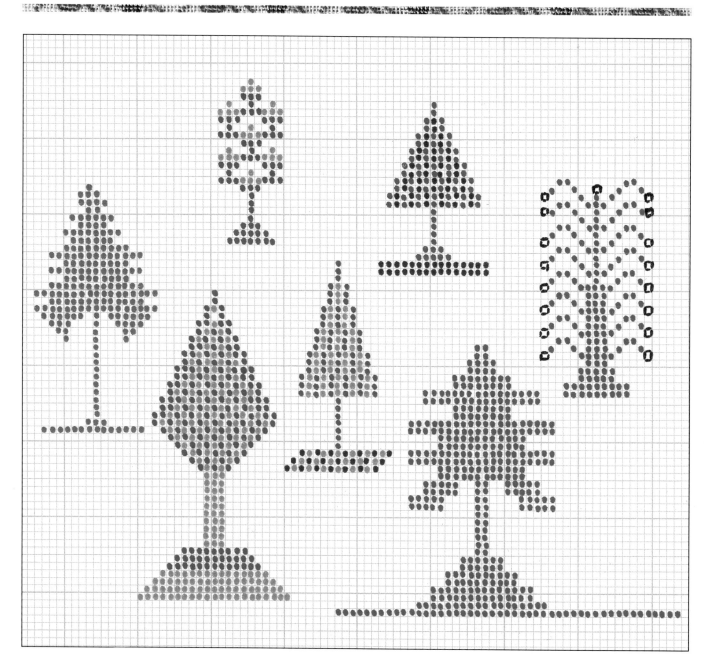

Trees appear in all shapes and sizes as motifs in sampler making but the most common is the biblical Tree of Knowledge which is generally shown as a stylized apple tree. Oak trees are a favoured motif and oak leaves and acorns feature in many decorative borders. Vine leaves and grapes are used both in borders and as motifs on band samplers. Many small trees appear in the 18th century following the fashion for topiary, the pruning and trimming of trees into ornamental shapes.

The scale of motifs whether they be fruit, flowers or trees has no relation to their actual size in nature. Trees are often dwarfed by the birds that sit in them and bowls of fruit or sprays of flowers figure larger than many animals. The motifs were adapted from all sorts of sources and rarely changed in size. When working a sampler today the same principals can apply: namely, if you like a particular motif then it can be added to your sampler without altering the proportions.

Included in this chapter are many floral motifs from different centuries of sampler making. They are all suitable to be used in a contemporary design and will work alongside your own ideas and motifs.

Above and right: *From 18th- and 19th-century European and American samplers, a selection of tree motifs. The apple trees with their luscious red fruits are traditionally associated with scenes depicting the temptation of Adam by Eve.*

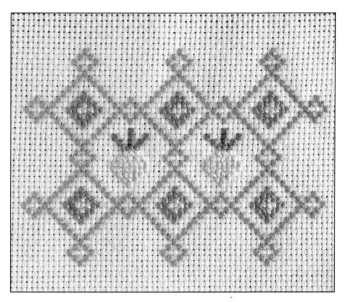

Left: *Strawberry pattern from 18th-century English sampler worked by Jane Rollistone Alleyne.*

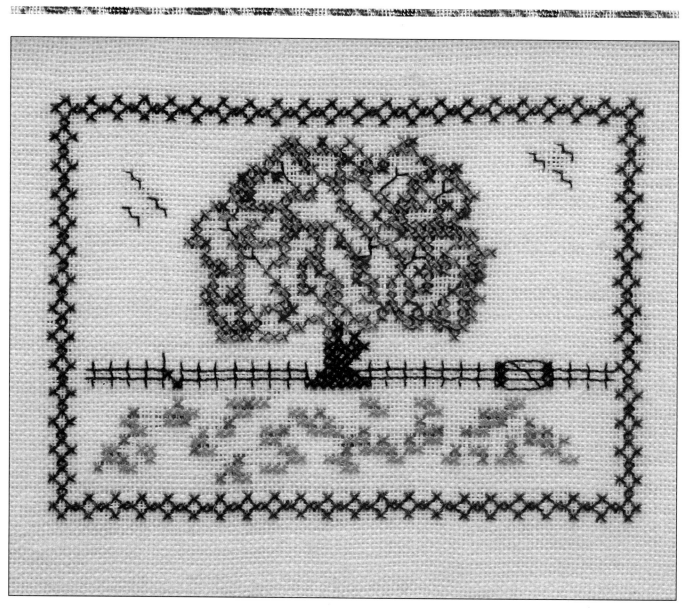

Above: *Tree in Field (13cm x 18cm/5in x 7in), a small contemporary sampler in cross stitch and running stitch which shows that samplers can also be very small with just one motif.*

Right: *Modern working of an old Danish wedding sampler with traditional bird, tree, fruit bowl and crown motifs.*

Left: House sampler worked in 1800 by Mary Ann Richards.

Below: Oak tree motif in cross stitch and double running stitch, and one unit of a rosebud and cornflower border which is repeated as necessary.

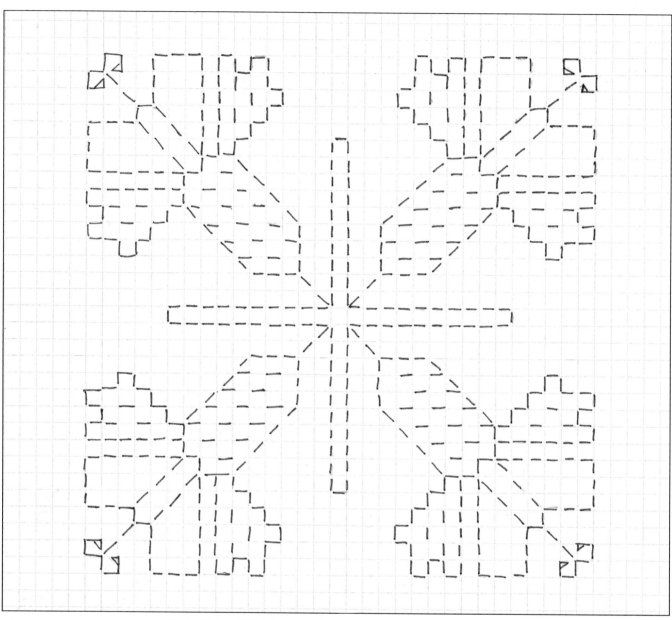

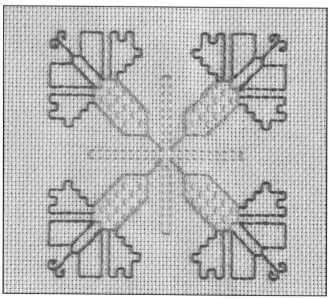

Above: *A carnation motif taken from a sampler dated 1598. These types of designs worked in Holbein stitch and running stitch are generally found on band samplers where the motif may be worked two or three times across the width of the sampler. It is most effective when worked in two colours and the scale of the design can be changed by altering the length of the running stitch which is a constant length throughout the motif. If the stitch is made longer the carnation will be enlarged; a shorter stitch will condense the pattern.*

Left: *Carnation pattern from a late 16th-century sampler worked in Holbein stitch with running stitch.*

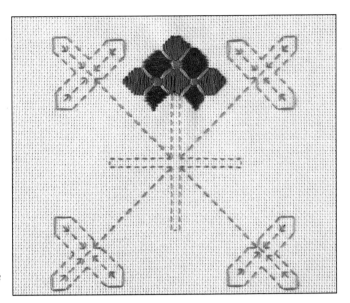

Left *A grape and vine leaf design taken from a band sampler. The fruit could be worked in different colours to suggest raspberries or blackberries. The outline and leaves have been worked in running stitch with the fruit in contrasting satin stitch where one section has been worked at right angles to the next to give an effect of light and shade. This makes the design more three dimensional.*

Below: *Vine leaf and grape motif from a late 16th-century English sampler.*

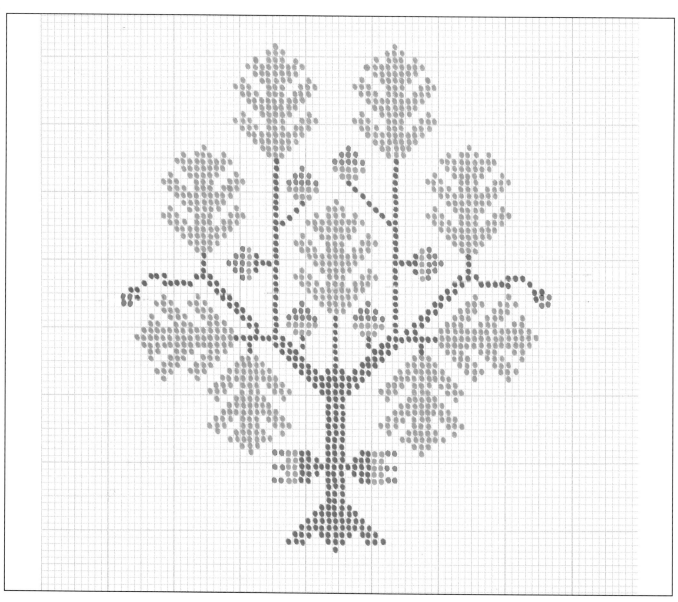

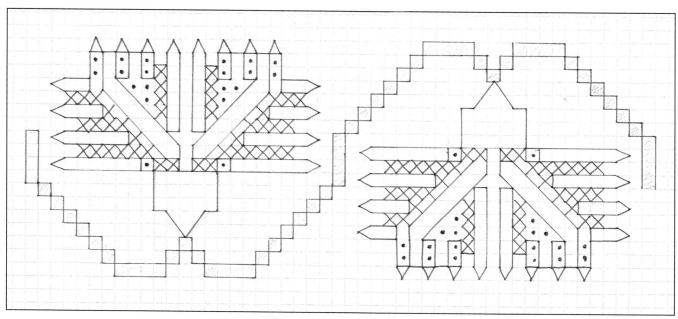

Opposite, above: *An oak tree with acorns taken from a sampler by Mary Smith worked in 1729. This makes a strong central motif for a small sampler or it could be worked as a pair on a larger piece of work. The design was originally worked in cross stitch and it was transferred onto graph paper straight from the sampler.*

Opposite, below: *A carnation motif ready to work in satin stitch, running stitch or cross stitch. It could also be worked in a combination of stitches, such as: running stitch for the outline of the flower, cross stitch for the centre, with French knots for the dots and satin stitch for the linking line.*

Above: *Lemon Tree (21cm × 19cm/8¼in × 7½in). Cross stitch on linen, a small sampler double mounted with a traditional acorn band pattern separating the two alphabets.*

ANIMALS, HOUSES AND PEOPLE

All sorts of animals can be found in samplers: from lions, stags and dogs to butterflies, beetles and frogs. In early samplers the animal motifs seem to have been derived from heraldic crests, as the stance of any particular animal tends to be the same as it would be in heraldry. This is probably due to the fact that the early samplers were worked by women of noble households so a family crest or emblem would have been a natural choice for a motif.

Later on the animals tend to be of the more domestic type, particularly when samplers are being worked by girls of all social classes as part of their education. Birds are by far the most common animals stitched in samplers and appear in all shapes and sizes. Everything from grand peacocks with their tails in pride to small doves and parrots. They are shown in flight, on the ground, in trees and sitting on the roofs of houses, especially country cottages. Different types of insects and beetles were popular during the 17th century but only butterflies survived as insect motifs into the 18th and 19th centuries. Animals were never as popular a choice as flowers for motifs and became less so when inscriptions and verses took over.

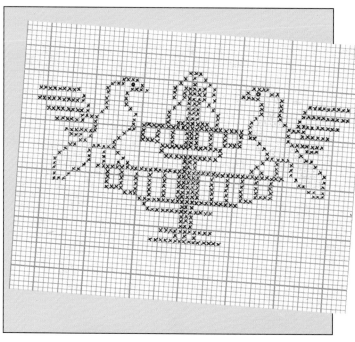

Opposite, top: *Birds at a fountain. This was very popular in Europe as a central motif. The design is ready to work in cross stitch.*

Opposite, centre: *A contemporary reworking of traditional bird motifs.*

Opposite, below left: *Detail of a peacock in pride, a bird motif much used in sampler making.*

Opposite, below right: *Peacock motif shown with its tail in pride.*

Left: *A selection of bird motifs. All sorts of birds are found in abundance in samplers. Illustrated here are the three main types: peacocks, parrots and doves.*

This page: *Drawings of two dragonflies and two beetles taken from an early 17th-century sampler. They were originally worked in tent stitch on fine linen canvas but could easily be worked in satin stitch and Holbein stitch.*

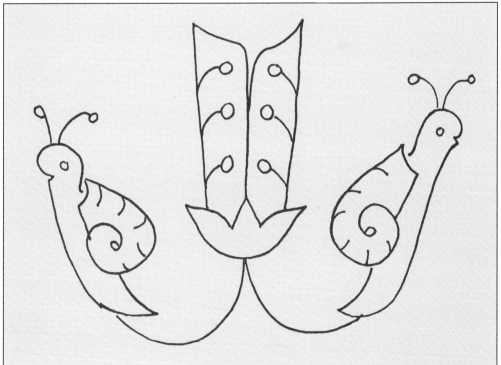

Above: *A selection of butterflies to work in cross stitch. These motifs are taken from 19th-century English and American samplers.*

Left: *Line drawings of snails on a pea pod taken from a 17th-century European pattern book. The design is ready to trace with the choice of stitches being left up to the embroiderer.*

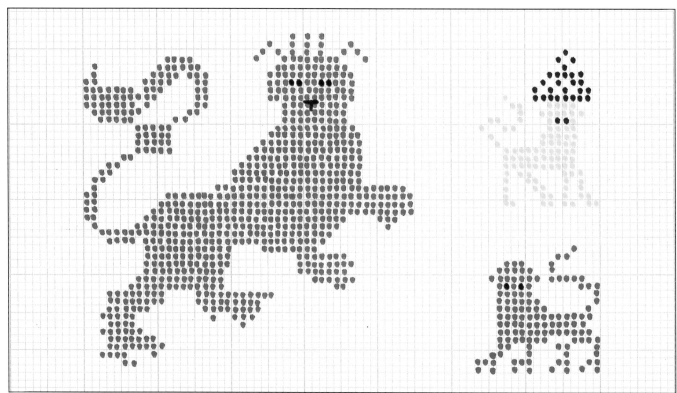

From the mid 18th century houses and buildings in general became more popular as subjects for samplers. Buildings with biblical associations, particularly Solomon's Temple, were favoured, as were royal palaces and mansions. Many of the houses have a uniformity of style which suggests that they were copied from pattern books or other samplers and they were generally stitched with a name above it to identify which particular building it was supposed to be.

There are examples of sampler makers depicting an actual house, as in Sophia Stephens' sampler of Horse Mill House, near London, but mostly they seem to be a picture of an idealized house. Cottages became more common as a subject in England in the 19th century particularly when placed in a rural setting. Windmills also make an appearance as a motif. This uniformity in style is restricted to the country of origin, where the styles are recognizably typical to each country. It is interesting to see how American samplers acquired their own style in this way, as people began to move away from their various European roots and evolve an independent cultural identity.

Opposite page: *An assortment of lions, dogs, cats and stags. The lion motifs were more popular in England and Europe and the style of the motifs derives from heraldic crests. The medieval fashion for emblazoning every surface with family crests spilled over into sampler making in Europe but in America domestic animals and stags were favourite motifs.*

Below: *House sampler (34cm × 40cm/13½in × 16in). A simple house and tree sampler with traditional peacock in pride motif with a mixed border of strawberries and flowers.*

Above: *English Village (32cm ×
37cm/12½in × 14½in). A sampler
showing the variety of buildings in a
small English village from the church
and pub to country cottage and
garden. The sampler is worked in cross
stitch and running stitch with beads
added for extra texture. Beads and
metallic threads are sometimes found
in European samplers but in America
from the mid-18th century all kinds of
extra fabrics and effects were used,
including paper cut outs as used in
découpage.*

Right: *Detail of church motif worked
in cross stitch on natural linen ground
fabric.*

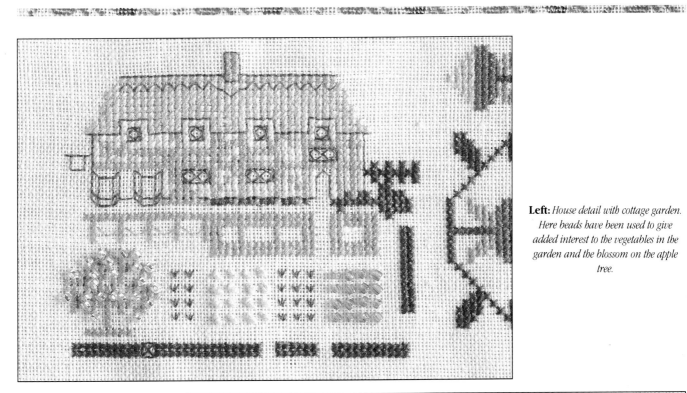

Left: *House detail with cottage garden. Here beads have been used to give added interest to the vegetables in the garden and the blossom on the apple tree.*

Right: *Country pub with duck pond and water pump worked in cross stitch with detail in running stitch. Building motifs became popular during the 18th century when local landmarks or important buildings were used as a central design for a sampler.*

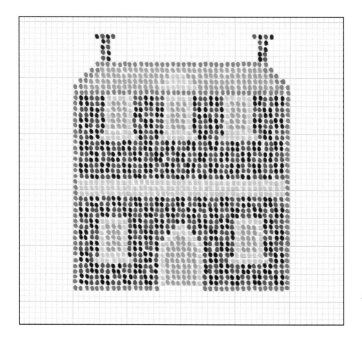

Right *A house motif which is taken from an early 19th century Pennsylvanian sampler. Many samplers included two or three buildings in a small piece of work.*

Below *This is Horse Mill House, near London, and was worked in cross stitch on the original sampler by Sophia Stephens in the 1830s.*

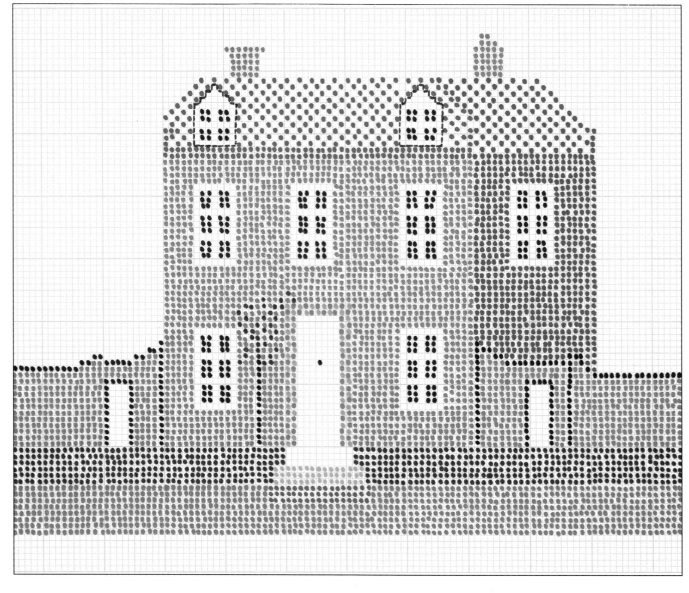

Above: *House sampler (21cm × 30cm/8¼in × 12in) showing an 18th-century style house motif with garden fence and trees, strawberry border and other assorted motifs. A gardener complete with spade is worked in the foreground. When working a sampler of your own home or family, all sorts of personal motifs could be added to identify each member of the family. For example a keen D.I.Y. enthusiast could be shown with a hammer in their hand or a tennis player with a racket.*

Left: *House motif worked in cross stitch with Holbein stitch detail. The stitches show up clearly enough to use the motif directly in your own designs. Before pattern books appeared in Europe in the 16th century the only means of enlarging your collection of patterns and motifs was to copy a design directly from another sampler.*

Opposite: *Little Red House sampler (13cm × 19cm/5in × 7½in), a charming and simple sampler worked in cross stitch and enhanced by a well-chosen frame.*

Left *This house motif was taken from a Pennsylvanian sampler dating from the early 1800s. Buildings in naturalistic landscapes were a particular favourite for American samplers.*

Below *This house motif was taken from an English sampler, where it was worked in cross stitch. You could try adding different stitches to create textures of bricks and tiles.*

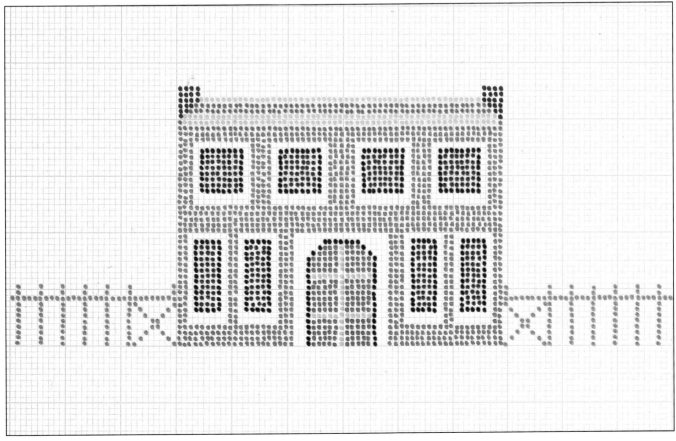

Above: *Church Sampler (29cm × 26cm/11½in × 10¼in). A modern sampler on a traditional theme with a building and flower case motif finished with a carnation border. The ground fabric is natural unbleached linen. Occasionally coloured linen was used in America and, for a short while, a fabric known as Linsey – woolsey. This was made by combining a blue/green warp thread of linen with a yellow-green woollen weft thread.*

People appear as motifs in samplers throughout every century and occur in all sorts of settings. They can however be generally placed in one of three distinct categories. Firstly there are the biblical figures which tend to feature in the earlier samplers. The most popular Bible story to be illustrated was that of Adam and Eve taking the fruit from the Tree of Knowledge but scenes from the life of Abraham and Jacob's dream were also popular images. Many of the pattern books included religious characters up to the end of the 17th century but from then on their popularity waned. Apart from Adam and Eve, who only have a fig leaf to cover their modesty, all the other biblical characters are shown dressed in costume that was contemporary for the date at

Opposite: *More figures and family groups to help personalize your samplers. These motifs are ready to work in cross stitch but you could add other details such as beads to the dress or a feather in the woman's hat.*

which the sampler was worked. This was a common practice through-out the medieval period and no attempt was ever made to make the dress of the characters historically accurate.

The second group of figure patterns generally includes family types and other individual people motifs such as shepherds and shepherd-esses. Some family samplers include every member of a family com-plete with their servants, dogs and cats. Others only depict one or two people as shown in a charming late 18th century sampler with a figure of a man in a frock coat and hat above whom the inscription reads 'THIS IS MY DEAR FATHER.' As with the biblical characters, these figures are clothed in costume that was fashionable for the time.

The last group are the more mysterious 'boxer figures'. These only really appear in the 17th century and their derivation is obscure. They are usually worked in pairs facing each other on either side of a floral motif. Their name refers to their customary stance, with one hand held aloft, which has been interpreted to mean that they are about to box with each other. They generally hold a flower or fruit in the uplifted hand. It is more likely that they represent a pair of lovers exchanging gifts or tokens of affection than men about to fight. In early examples they are stitched with no clothes on which tends to give credence to the 'lovers' theory but gradually clothes were added, in particular the breeches, which gave them their characteristic boxer appearance.

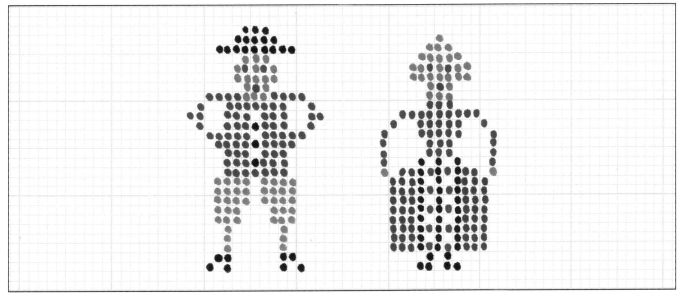

Right: *Figure detail of a woman with a spinning wheel.*

Below: *A figure of a man taken from a late 18th century English sampler which had the inscription above of THIS IS MY DEAR FATHER. The stitching on the original sampler was quite crude and was obviously made by a very young girl who nevertheless has made a charming portrait of her father.*

Below: *'Boxer' figure popular in Europe through the 17th century, here shown nude with a typical trophy or flower motif in the uplifted hand. Later on these figures acquired breeches and should you wish to add these simply work the area between the two shaded lines in a darker shade and add white socks and black shoes to the feet.*

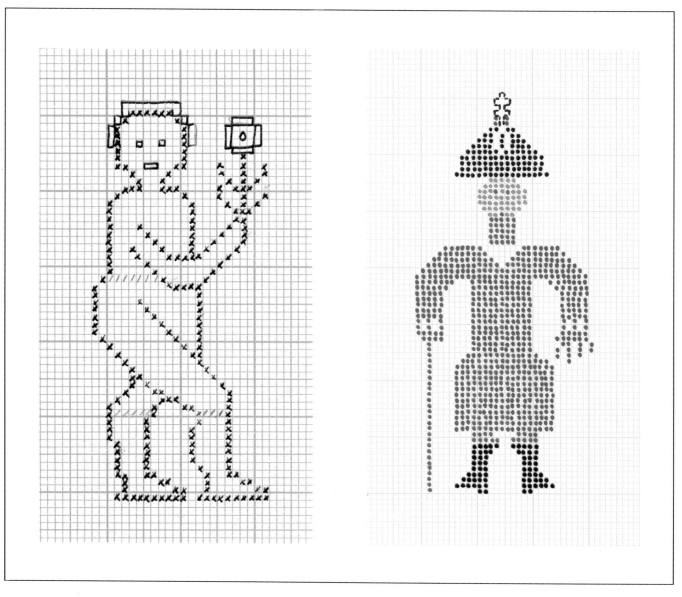

Above: *House sampler by Mary Pether finished in 1839. Worked in silk thread on a fine wool ground with* *naturalistic house, garden and dress detail with the ever present over-sized fruit and flower bowls.*

Left: *Boxer Sampler (20cm × 38cm/8in × 15in). A traditional band sampler from 1698 updated and reworked in 1987 by Jane Greenoff. The boxer motif has been turned around to face forwards which makes them appear alarmed rather than aggressive.*

Below: *Detail of a re-worked 17th-century boxer sampler where the figures have been turned to face the front. The hunting bounds are typical of the late 17h century and are a popular motif for samplers up to the present day.*

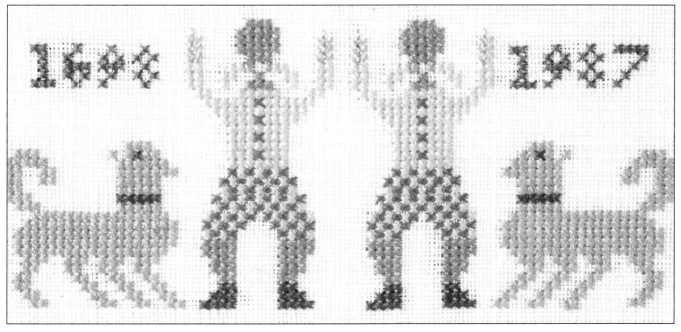

ALPHABETS, NUMBERS AND VERSES

In early samplers numbers and letters were only used to record the date on which the work was finished and by whom it had been made. Verses and prayers from the Bible were sometimes used but it was not until the 18th century that the fashion for alphabets began in earnest. Once the sampler ceased to be a personal book of patterns and stitches and became a means of educating small girls, alphabets and numbers begin to dominate the design. Not only did young girls learn

to sew with a sampler but also to read, write, and count.

The size of cloth generally dictated the size and spacing of the letters in an alphabet or verse. Quite often there seems to be a miscalculation with the spacing and the letters can get more squashed towards the end of a row. Some letters were left out entirely, either by mistake or miscalculation, although J and U were little used before the 19th century, I and V being used in their place. Numerals appear in the 17th century as a complete row of digits from 0–9 although later on any amount of numbers from 1–24 can be worked. They are mostly worked in a single row underneath an alphabet.

From the 18th century onwards samplers become full of inscriptions and verses that concern themselves with the virtues of obedience, duty,

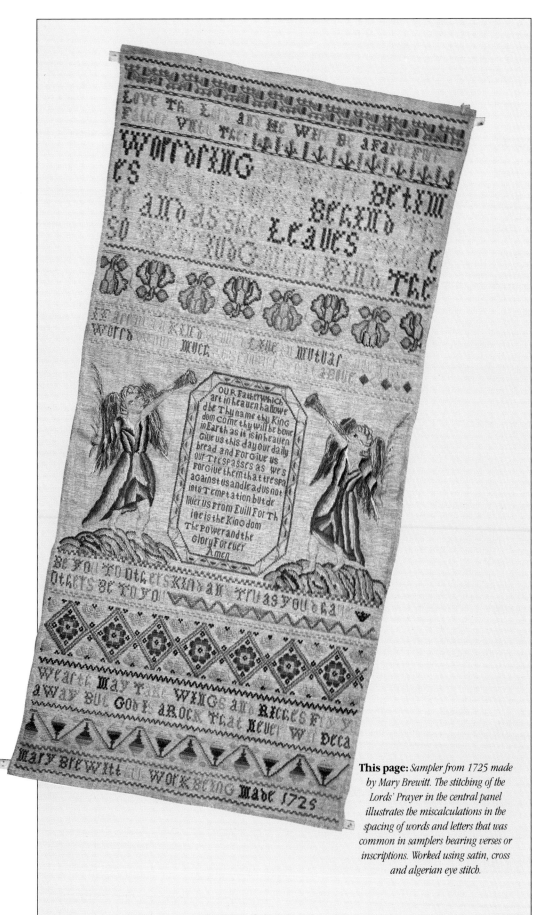

This page: *Sampler from 1725 made by Mary Brewitt. The stitching of the Lords' Prayer in the central panel illustrates the miscalculations in the spacing of words and letters that was common in samplers bearing verses or inscriptions. Worked using satin, cross and algerian eye stitch.*

Opposite page: *Patience (23cm × 23cm/9in × 9in). A motto sampler with traditional spot and band motifs worked in soft tones of green, blue and beige. Old samplers are worked with threads coloured with natural vegetable dyes which gives them a much softer and more subtle colouring. This effect can be achieved by using close tones of one colour when using chemically dyed commercial yarns.*

Below: *Crowns and numbers. Numerals, like letters, appear in samplers throughout Europe and America and were used primarily for marking household linen.*

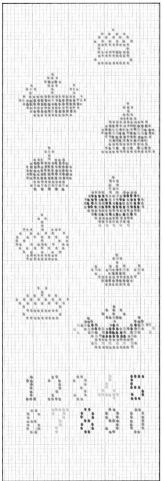

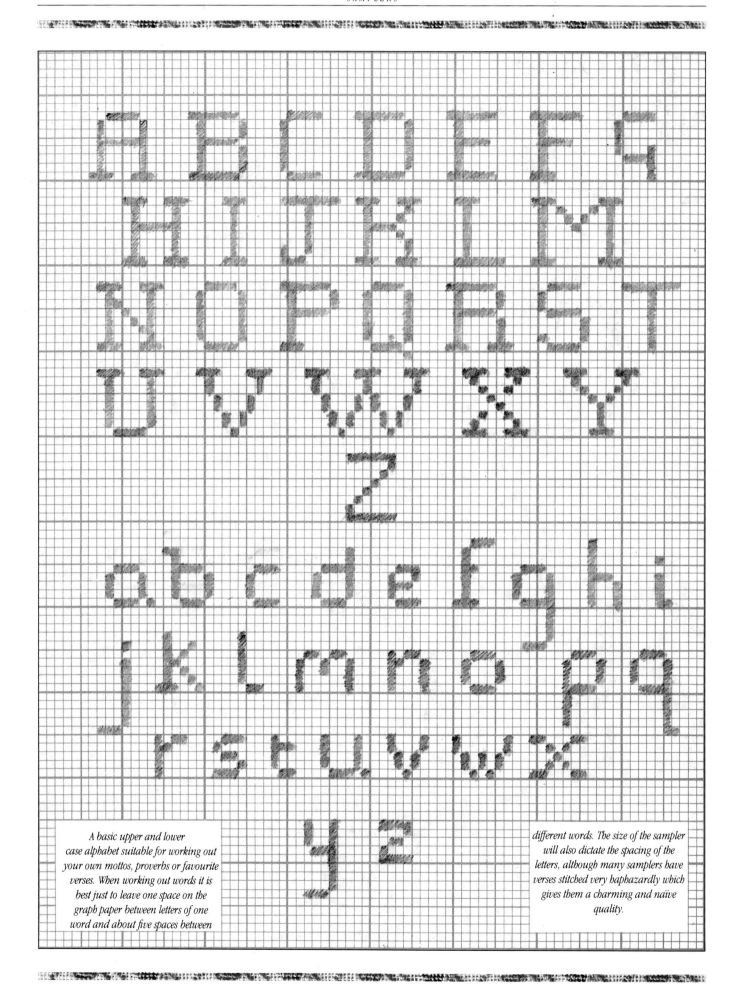

A basic upper and lower case alphabet suitable for working out your own mottos, proverbs or favourite verses. When working out words it is best just to leave one space on the graph paper between letters of one word and about five spaces between different words. The size of the sampler will also dictate the spacing of the letters, although many samplers have verses stitched very haphazardly which gives them a charming and naïve quality.

Full upper case alphabet which can be used as a decorative element in a sampler. The letters could also be used as fancy capitals at the beginning of a name or motto.

learning and humility; there are endless variations on these themes. Girls also stitched eulogies for their friends and acknowledgements to their parents. One of the more charming being stitched by Ann Waiters.

'Ann Waiters is my name and with
my needle I mark the same
That all my friends may plainly
see what care my parents took of me'.

Or in another sampler dated June 7th 1700 Prisca Philips stitched this moral tale and acknowledged her teacher,

Prisca Philips — Look well
to what you take
in hand for larning
is better than house or
land when land is gone
and money spent then
larning is most excellent. June 7 1700
Iudeth Hayl
was my mist
ris.

Right: *Detail of a verse worked simply in running stitch with pansy motifs worked in cross stitch.*

Opposite page: *'She Seeketh' sampler (29cm × 39cm/11½in × 15½in). Eight close tones of earth colours worked on a dark natural linen ground with motto and spot motifs.*

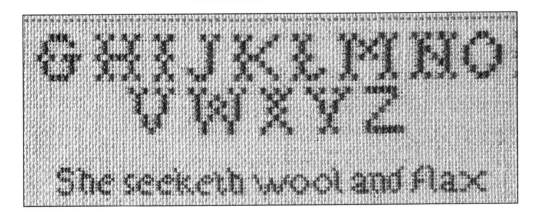

Left: *Detail of the motto from a contemporary sampler.*

Although many a sampler records how hard the 'larning' was as Elizabeth Clements stitches in 1712:

> *This I have done I thank my God without the*
> *Correction of the rod. Elizabeth Clements.*

The motto *'Be not weary in well doing'* was often stitched at the end of a sampler, sometimes it featured half way down as if to encourage the faint-hearted.

During the 19th century the verses have an increasing preoccupation with death and the samplers are all the more poignant for being stitched by very young girls. Margaret Morgan aged 14 in 1839 stitched:

> *There is an hour when I must die*
> *Nor can I tell how soon will come*
> *A thousand children young as I*
> *Are called by death to hear their doom.*

Another girl aged 7 stitched these lines,

> *And now my soul another year*
> *Of thy short life is past*
> *I cannot long continue here*
> *And this may be my last.*

Verses and inscriptions get increasingly longer until complete poems are being worked in embroidery but not all girls adhered to the moral tone expected in their work. One of the most charming inscriptions, which sums up the spirit of sampler making, is from an unsigned and undated sampler that simply states,

> *Here a figure there a letter*
> *One done bad the other better.*

Another useful outlet for girls' sewing and writing ability was in the marking of household linen. During the 17th century the increasing general prosperity resulted in many households stockpiling extra linen. Girls who had proved their competence in a sampler, were employed in the task of marking the endless sheets, pillowcases and towels. Generally the marking involved a simple set of initials with some identifying number but in grander houses in Europe the relevant rank of nobility was also used. Girls were taught patterns to represent crowns and coronets and how to distinguish between all the different ranks from the king down to a baron. Naturally in America the marking was much more domestically orientated as rank was much less significant and the motifs to denote it were therefore used much less frequently. However, these crown patterns became popular in samplers and were often added in for decorative purposes or placed in borders.

Right: *House and Alphabet (13cm × 18cm/5in × 7in). Another small sampler with two main motifs and an alphabet worked in running stitch.*

Below: *Wings of Friendship (13cm × 18cm/5in × 7in). A small motto sampler worked in cross stitch and running stitch. A detail from a larger piece of work make excellent small samplers like this one.*

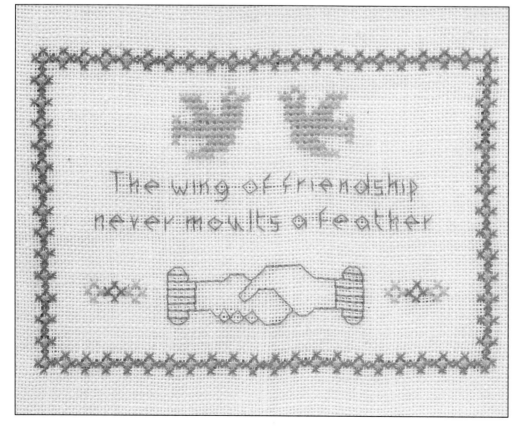

Right: *Silver Wedding Sampler (32cm × 27cm/13in × 10½in). A more contemporary subject to commemorate in a sampler, this one is worked in cross stitch with details such as the wedding bells worked in silver thread. A similar sampler could be worked to mark a golden wedding.*

Above: *Sampler worked by Lydia Oldham in 1825. A good example of an alphabet sampler showing different typefaces. This is also a good illustration of how children were taught their numbers and letters through working samplers as well as learning to embroider.*

Opposite page: *Alphabet Sampler (25cm × 17cm/10in × 6¾in). You could try collecting alphabets and working each new one into a strip or band sampler which would be an ideal gift for a child. The sampler shown here has been simply finished off with the ever-popular strawberry border.*

BORDERS AND PATTERNS

The early band samplers were not given borders but once the shape changed to the square form borders started to appear. With a square sampler, which is more of a picture, the border becomes a useful way of framing the design. However, borders evolved gradually. They started off as just a simple band design stitched across the top or bottom of the work, sometimes only the two vertical sides have the borders worked. Naturally enough the border soon became one design worked around the sampler to frame the central verse or motif.

The patterns for borders were nearly always worked up from fruit or flower motifs with occasional geometric or simple running designs. The strawberry motif, especially the fruit, is by far the most popular choice of design for a border and it is still very common in samplers worked today.

Included in this section are many designs for borders that have been derived from examples found in old samplers. Should you wish to make up your own borders then the simple repetition of one or two motifs, as in the cross and tree design, makes a very effective pattern. Another method for creating a border is to take two compatible motifs and link them together with a stepped line, as in the rose and carnation border. The combinations of motifs are endless and a sampler could be worked with a different border at the top and bottom to the two sides, or four separate borders could be worked so that each edge was different.

Opposite: *Decorative fruit and floral borders from the mid-19th century.*

Left: *From Elizabeth Turner's sampler made in 1771, a border of carnations and roses.*

Below: *Patterns from a band sampler worked in running stitch. The stitches are clear enough to work the designs direct from the photograph and the patterns simple enough to work your own variations on the themes.*

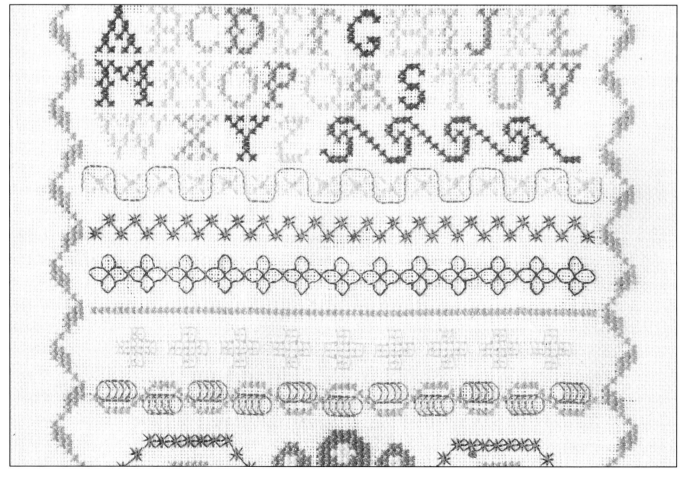

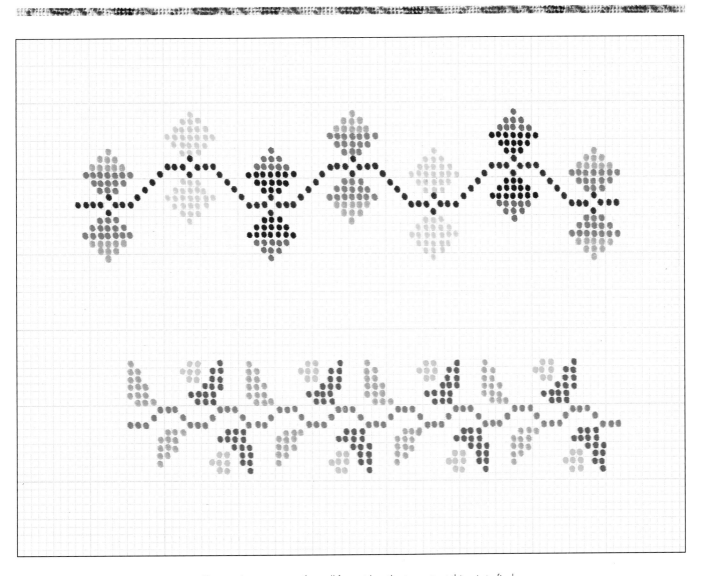

If using the same motif on all four sides, the important thing is to find the centre of the pattern and the centre of the edge to be worked, and ensuring that the two coincide. Then the corners can be worked out by placing a mirror at 45° to the right part of the design and drawing out the resulting right-angled border onto graph or plain paper as appropriate. It is then ready to use on the sampler.

Corners

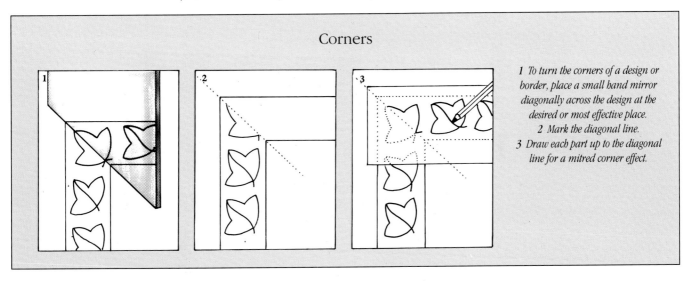

1 To turn the corners of a design or border, place a small hand mirror diagonally across the design at the desired or most effective place.
2 Mark the diagonal line.
3 Draw each part up to the diagonal line for a mitred corner effect.

Above: *This chart shows examples of patterns arranged for corners.*

Above: *A worked sample of the chart,
showing how one square is used to
indicate one stitch.*

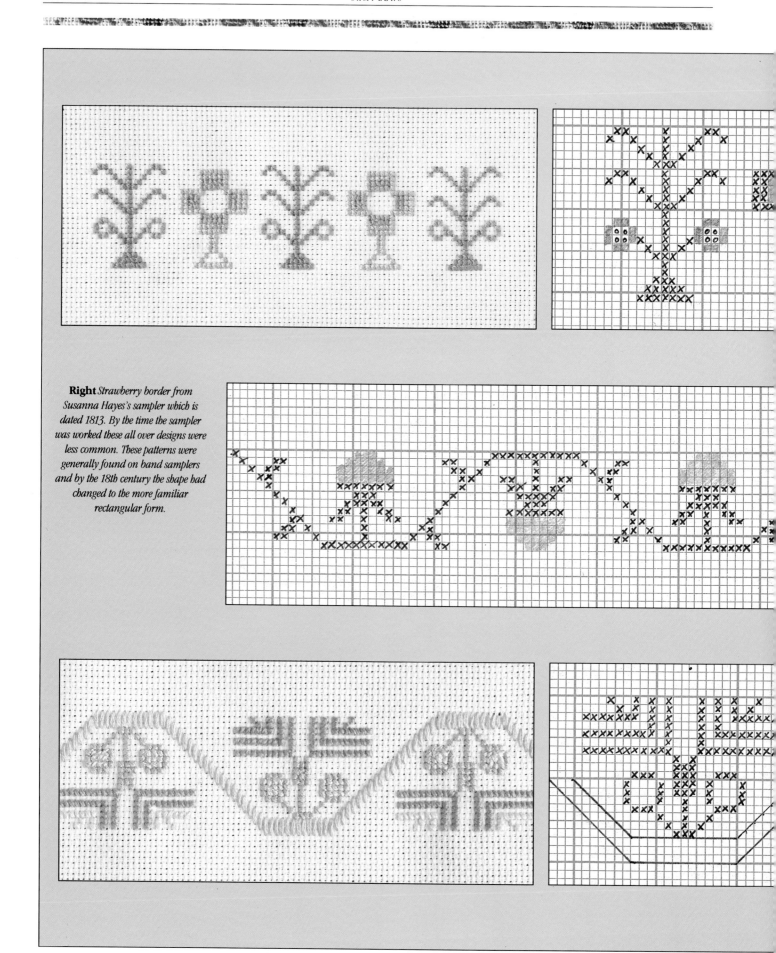

Right *Strawberry border from Susanna Hayes's sampler which is dated 1813. By the time the sampler was worked these all over designs were less common. These patterns were generally found on band samplers and by the 18th century the shape had changed to the more familiar rectangular form.*

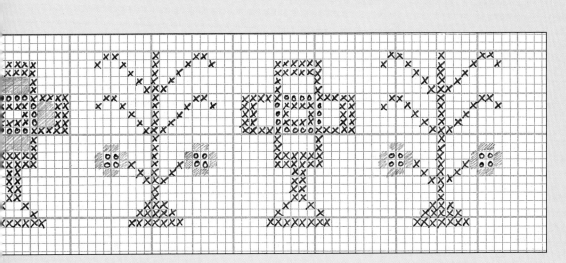

Left *Cross and Tree Border from Mary Heavside's sampler, worked in 1735. The two motifs could be used separately.*

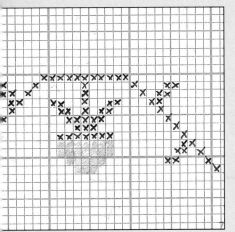

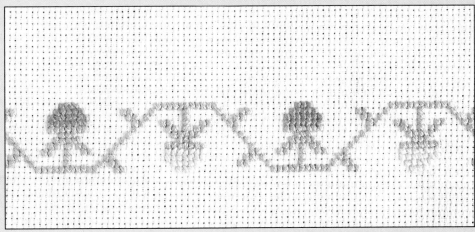

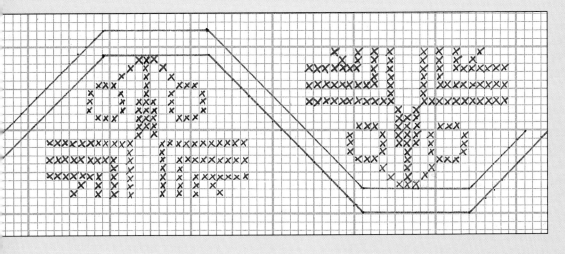

Left *Carnation border pattern from Margaret Knowle's sampler finished in 1738. This pattern was popular throughout Europe and America; here the design has been flattened out to become a more abstract motif.*

Right: *The ever-popular strawberry border. This example is taken from an English sampler but strawberries were used in borders on samplers throughout Europe and America and is still the most popular fruit motif used today.*

Below: *Grape and Vine border pattern. With this design it is a challenge to make each bunch different, which makes a lively and effective border.*

Opposite, top: *A carnation border of the early 19th century that assumes a more naturalistic form. American borders tended to be more naturalistic and full of floral motifs that quite often dwarfed the central design.*

Opposite, centre: *A simple rose border pattern taken from a sampler worked by Catherine Pickling in 1780. In this design the colour of the petals in the first rose becomes the centre of the next rose and so on. This idea could be repeated indefinitely so that each rose was completely different from all the rest. Here the design is worked with a repeat after four colour changes.*

Opposite, bottom: *A mid-19th-century border pattern of oranges. By changing the colour of the fruit this could become a border of plums, peaches or apricots.*

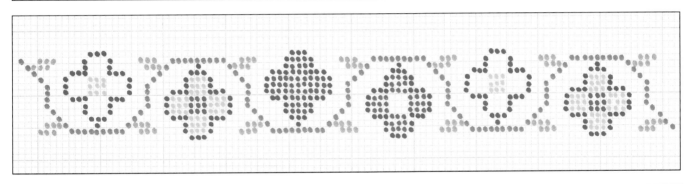

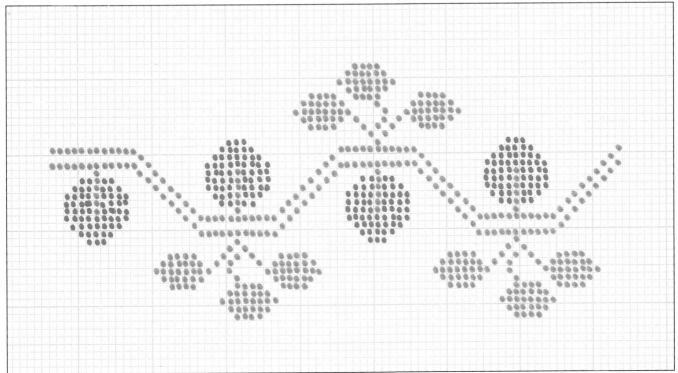

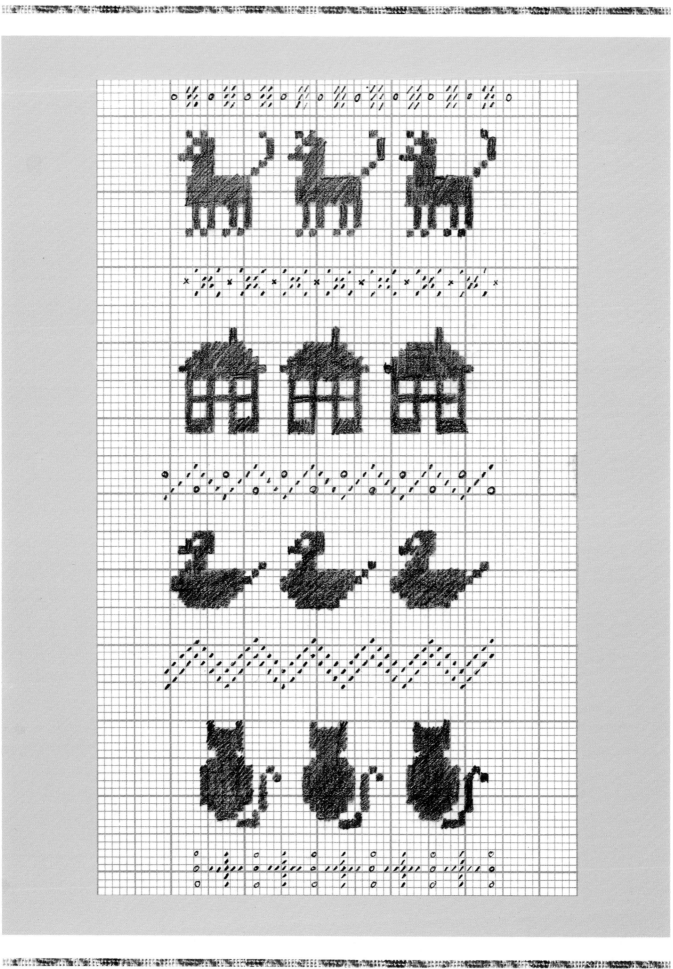

Left: *Honeysuckle and rose border pattern from Sara Carr's sampler, dated 1809.*

Opposite page: *A selection of contemporary designs to be used in borders or as individual motifs when designing your own samplers.*

Below: *Rose and Carnation borders. These motifs have always been popular from the earliest samplers to the present day. They were used in both European and American samplers and found extensively in borders. The rose is shown in its early form, which is also referred to as the Tudor rose. This example was taken from a sampler made in the late 18th century.*

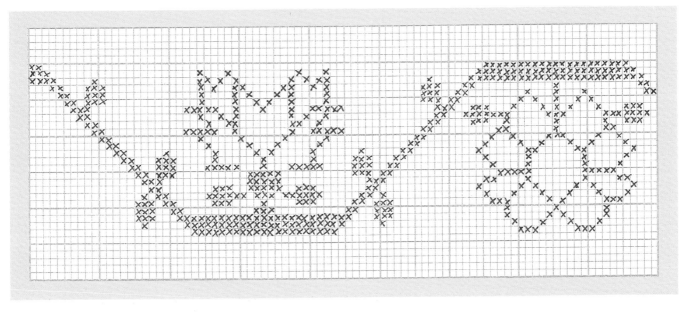

BLOCKING, MOUNTING AND FRAMING

A piece of embroidery or canvas work may become distorted whilst it is being worked and if this happens it should be blocked when finished to help it regain its original shape. If the embroidery has been worked on plain or even weave fabric with a frame then the piece should not be very distorted, if at all. Likewise, with canvas work that has been properly stretched in a frame, the distortion should be minimal. If this is the case then the embroidery or canvas will need only a simple pressing. Once it has been blocked or pressed the piece can then be framed.

◆ Pressing ◆

Lay the piece of embroidery on a towel on a flat surface or ironing board with the right side downwards. Cover the work with a cloth and gently iron over the top or better still put a shot of steam through the layers of fabric. This should press the fabric but not flatten the stitches.

◆ Blocking ◆

Canvaswork tends to need blocking more than embroidery due to the fact that the most common canvaswork stitch, tent stich, is diagonal in structure. To block a piece of work dampen it with a spray or wet sponge and place face upwards on a wooden board. Position a tack in the centre of the top edge of unworked canvas and fix into the

Above: *Country Cottage (22cm × 17cm/8¾in × 6¾in). A small sampler that is double mounted for extra effect, with the window frame covered in linen and another related motif worked on the fabric covered mount. This idea could be further developed with two or three layers of* linen-covered window mounts, each with different motifs, set in a deeply rebated frame.

Opposite page: *Finished samplers framed and displayed on a wall give a personal touch to any room.*

board. Gently pull and straighten the vertical threads of the canvas and tack down the centre of the bottom edge. Repeat this process with the horizontal threads keeping them at right angles to the vertical threads. Working outwards from these four points, tack down the edges of the canvas so that the piece is held firmly in the correct shape. Allow to dry naturally and away from direct sunlight. Do not remove from the board until it is completely dry all over or it can become distorted again. If it does become distorted or if the initial blocking did not straighten it out completely, repeat the blocking process until the right shape is achieved.

◆ Framing ◆

To protect a piece of embroidery from dirt or damage by moths and insects it is advisable to frame it behind glass. Before framing the piece it must be mounted on either a stretcher, sheet of hardboard or museum board.

To mount the piece of embroidery lay it face down on a flat surface. Place the stretcher or board over the embroidery and fold over the unworked edges. With a stretcher tack down the edges making sure that the piece is properly stretched and all the threads lie straight up

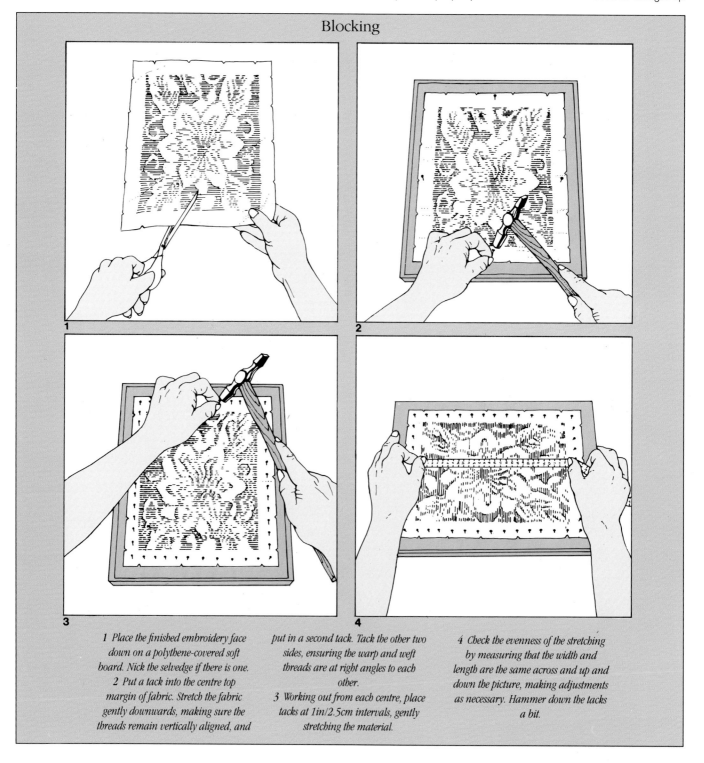

Blocking

1 Place the finished embroidery face down on a polythene-covered soft board. Nick the selvedge if there is one.
2 Put a tack into the centre top margin of fabric. Stretch the fabric gently downwards, making sure the threads remain vertically aligned, and

put in a second tack. Tack the other two sides, ensuring the warp and weft threads are at right angles to each other.
3 Working out from each centre, place tacks at 1in/2.5cm intervals, gently stretching the material.

4 Check the evenness of the stretching by measuring that the width and length are the same across and up and down the picture, making adjustments as necessary. Hammer down the tacks a bit.

Mounting and lacing

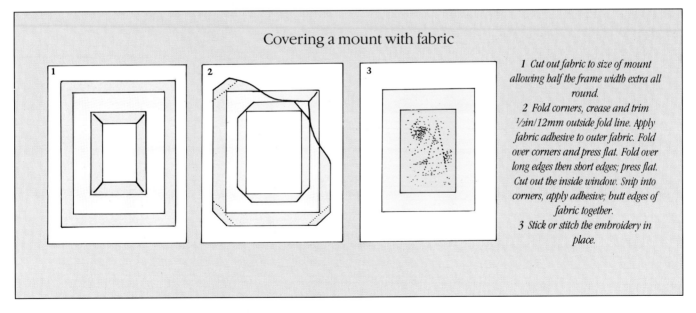

To lace an embroidery over a wooden or cardboard block, begin by first establishing the exact area of the final panel. Using two L-shaped pieces of card, cover the raw edges keeping the straight grain if possible. Mark the corners with pins and tack out the shape. Cut a piece of hardboard, cardboard or softboard, a little smaller than the tacked line. Place the card on the wrong side, inside the tacked line. Secure with pins inserted into the edges of the card (1). Using a long length of strong thread, lace across working from the centre out and pulling thread tight (2). Complete second half (3). Repeat vertically, lacing under and over the horizontal threads working from the centre again (4). Check that the front is still correct; adjust if necessary. Trim corner to remove bulk. Complete the lacing (5). Cut out a piece of fabric to cover the back. Turn edges under and neatly stitch down.

Covering a mount with fabric

1 Cut out fabric to size of mount allowing half the frame width extra all round.

2 Fold corners, crease and trim 1/2in/12mm outside fold line. Apply fabric adhesive to outer fabric. Fold over corners and press flat. Fold over long edges then short edges; press flat. Cut out the inside window. Snip into corners, apply adhesive; butt edges of fabric together.

3 Stick or stitch the embroidery in place.

and down or across the piece. The corners should be mitred and tacked firmly into place. With board, the edges should be laced together at the back. Pin the unworked fabric securely to the edges of the board. Starting with the top and bottom edges lace them together using a herringbone stitch, pull the stitches tight so that there is no give in the fabric. Then lace the two vertical sides together in the same way.

Once the piece has been mounted it can then be placed in a frame. It is important that the surface of the embroidery does not touch the glass and to prevent this a window mount should be placed between the work and the glass.

Unless you are skilled at framing, this last stage of the job is best left to a specialist.

This page: *Framed finished samplers of all sizes and types can be grouped together to make an effective display.*

Glossary

Aida cloth An even-weave fabric with a regular number of holes to the inch. Suitable for counted thread work and particularly useful when working cross stitch designs.

band sampler An early form of the sampler worked on a long thin strip of linen. The designs were usually worked in horizontal bands across the width of the fabric.

Berlin woolwork A method of working designs from a printed chart in coloured wools on a cotton canvas background. The designs originated in Germany but became very popular in Europe and America.

Binca fabric An even-weave fabric with regular squares formed by the warp and weft threads, suitable for coarse embroidery or beginners.

boxer A 17th-century embroidery motif initially shown as a nude figure with a token or gift in an uplifted hand, now thought to represent lovers. They were gradually clothed and assumed the name boxer because of their seemingly aggressive stance.

canvas A woven ground fabric for embroidery where the warp and weft threads interlock to produce precisely spaced holes. Canvas comes in a wide variety of gauges.

coton à broder A pearlized cotton thread, tightly twisted with a sheen finish.

couching A method of tying down a thread onto the ground fabric by stitching over it with another thread at regular intervals. This is a particularly suitable method for using thick, textured or metallic threads in embroidery.

double canvas Canvas where the holes are spaced between pairs of vertical and horizontal threads. Useful for very fine detailed work.

embroidery frame (hoop) A round frame for stretching the ground fabric before commencing embroidery. It keeps the fabric under an even tension and helps prevent puckering or distortions.

gauge The number of threads within a given distance ie 1 inch/2.5cm that can be stitched over or embroidered. Used in relation to canvas and even-weave fabrics.

graph paper Paper printed with a grid or regular sized squares used to chart a design before it is worked.

ground fabric The background fabric for any piece of embroidery.

Hardanger An open weave double thread linen background fabric originating in Norway.

motif A single unit of design used on its own as a feature or repeated to form borders or an all over pattern.

needlepoint A general term for embroidery worked on canvas.

opus anglicanum A term that refers to ecclesiastical embroidery produced in England between the 12th and 14th centuries.

pattern book A printed book of designs produced specifically for the use of embroiderers.

pearl cotton A twisted two-ply embroidery thread with a high sheen finish. Available as a single thread in different thicknesses.

pictorial sampler A sampler where separate motifs form a picture. More popular in America during the 18th and 19th centuries.

plain weave fabric A ground fabric where the warp and weft threads are not regularly spaced, as in even-weave, but the fabric has a smooth surface suitable for embroidery

single canvas Canvas where the holes are spaced between single interlocking vertical and horizontal threads.

spot sampler A sampler where the motifs are worked singly and placed anywhere on the fabric in order to show off or record a wide variety of stitches and techniques.

stranded cotton A six-strand cotton thread with a shiny finish suitable for all types of embroidery. The threads can be sub-divided to create different thicknesses of yarn.

tailor's chalk A soft chalk used to mark fabric before sewing. Used in embroidery to outline motifs and shapes. Marks can be removed by brushing the chalk off the surface of the fabric with a brush.

tammy cloth A woollen cloth especially woven as a ground fabric for sampler making, most popular in the 18th century.

Bibliography

English Secular Embroidery – M Jourdain 1910
Floral Symbolism of the Great Masters – Elizabeth Haig 1913
Samplers and Tapestry Embroideries – M B Huish 1913
English Needlework – A F Kendrick 1933
Guide to collection of samplers and embroideries, National Museum of Wales – F G Payne 1939
Samplers – Averil Colby 1964
A Gallery of American Samplers – Glee Krueger – E P Dutton 1978
Cross Stitch and Sampler Book – Jan Eaton & Liz Mundle 1985
The Subversive Stitch, exhibition catalogue – Whitworth Art Gallery 1988